AFTER ABUSE

Papers on
caring and planning
for a child
who has been
sexually abused

BRITISH AGENCIES FOR
ADOPTION & FOSTERING

Published by British Agencies for Adoption & Fostering
11 Southwark Street, London SE1 1RQ

© BAAF 1989
ISBN 0 903534 82 7
Designed by Andrew Haig
Typeset by Ethnographica
Printed in England

Contents

About the authors

Arnon Bentovim is Consultant Psychiatrist at the Hospitals for Sick Children, Great Ormond Street, and the Tavistock Clinic in London. He is also a Chairman of the Institute of Family Therapy.

Anne Elton is Principal Psychiatric Social Worker at the Hospitals for Sick Children, Great Ormond Street and a member of the Barclay Committee on Social Work and of the Institute of Family Therapy.

Barbara Jones is employed by Norfolk County Council as a Senior Social Worker with a Child Sexual Abuse Team. In 1987 and 1988 she was jointly awarded a Kellmer Pringle bursary to pursue the development of training materials for carers of sexually abused children.

Helen Kenward is a Principal Social Worker monitoring child abuse in Northamptonshire. She worked with the BBC as Social Work Adviser on *Childwatch* and with the police on training in joint investigations.

Jean La Fontaine is a freelance consultant and researcher. She was previously Professor of Anthropology at the London School of Economics.

Maria Mars is a Child Psychologist in the Psychology Service, Haringey Social Services, specialising in work with black families.

Kala Nobbs is a Fostering Officer with Norfolk County Council. She has worked with NFCA developing services for adolescents and in 1987/1988 was jointly awarded a Kellmer Pringle award for work in fostering sexually abused children. She now runs workshops on this subject for both foster parents and trainers.

Gerrilyn Smith is a Clinical Psychologist. She is currently on leave of absence from Haringey Social Services to lecture and organise the DHSS Postgraduate Training in Child Sexual Abuse at the Institute of Child Health, University of London.

Jacquie Roberts is Project Head of Polepark Family Counselling Centre, Dundee, which is a special centre set up to help abused neglected children and their families. She was previously a Family Finder at Lambeth Social Services Department.

Marianne Tranter is a Psychiatric Social Worker at the Hospitals for Sick Children, Great Ormond Street. She was formerly a field social worker in Islington.

Child sexual abuse: an ESRC research briefing

Professor Jean La Fontaine

Introduction

Public concern over the sexual abuse of children is a relatively recent phenomenon. Until 1980 the problem was not even mentioned in DHSS circulars.[1] Very little relevant research has yet been published, despite the large number of writings on the sexual abuse of children. There is research in progress but current discussions mostly rely on findings from research in the United States or on generalisations drawn from a few cases. Neither of these procedures is appropriate; until the American studies have been repeated here it would be unwise to assume that they hold for this society, which differs from that of the United States in many ways. Findings based on a few cases are of doubtful validity, since their representative nature cannot be established and control samples are all too often lacking.

Even the published research on the problem must be read with care. There is no standardised definition of the subject matter. The common use of the label 'child sexual abuse' conceals the different meanings which may be attached to it. The definitions affect the results of research. Estimates of the prevalence of sexual abuse vary from 54 per cent[2] to three per cent.[3] Although differences in the methods used may account for some of the difference between these two figures, one cannot say that one is more accurate than the other. The discrepancy between them is largely a matter of the definition of child sexual abuse that has been used. The particular meaning attached to the term may also affect conclusions as to whether children are more at risk outside or inside their homes (see below under 'Patterns of sexual abuse'.)

The sexual abuse of children is surrounded by a secrecy that makes it unusually difficult to study. All authorities on the subject report that the pressures on victims to remain silent or to retract their stories are heavy; threats of violence are not uncommon. A BBC questionnaire survey of self-selected adults found that 60 per cent of them claimed never to have told anyone. Nash and West's study of young women patients of a Cambridge practice[2] recorded 142 respondents to the 223 questionnaires as stating that they had not been abused. Seventy eight of those 142 were interviewed and 13 of them (17 per cent) revealed at the interview that they had in fact been abused. It is clear that only a proportion of cases are ever revealed; the research to show if these cases differ from those that are kept secret, and how, has yet to be done.

This paper was originally published as an ESRC Research Briefing in January 1988 and is reprinted here with permission.

The idea that children fantasise or tell lies about having been abused has been abandoned by much of the psychiatric community[4] but is still influential outside it. Children are often disregarded when they tell an adult what happened to them (see 'Studies of professionals' below). Gorry's study of incest reported to the Metropolitan Police[5] shows that only 25 per cent of the victims had made no attempt to tell. The others had not been believed. In over a third of the cases the person told had been a member of the child's family. Yet in only five per cent of the cases was the report of incest discovered to be unfounded and, in the illustrative example of such incidents described by Gorry, the informant was an adult, not a child. A common characteristic of child abusers is their refusal to accept responsibility for their actions; denials by parents are common even where there is good evidence to the contrary.

The scope of the problem

An early attempt to establish both the number of cases per year (incidence) and the proportion of the population affected (prevalence) in Great Britain was made by Mrazek, Lynch and Bentovim.[1] A postal survey of general practitioners, paediatricians, child psychiatrists and police surgeons asked for details of cases seen between June 1977 and May 1978. A limited number of professionals were approached and the response rate was not high (39 per cent). Even so, the total number of cases seen in the specified year was 1,072. Based on this sum, the authors suggested an annual incidence of 1,500 cases, or 1 in 6,000 children affected. Even on their own figures, this is a very conservative estimate; their estimated prevalence rate of 0.3 per cent of the population over childhood has subsequently been shown to be very much too low. Nash and West's rate of 48 per cent (the average of the rates for each of their two samples) seems very high but their definition of sexual abuse includes a wide variety of experiences; in about 19 per cent of their cases, there was only a single event.[2] However, it is not incompatible with Russell's San Francisco study[6] which did not use quite such a comprehensive definition but produced a prevalence rate of 38 per cent of adult women.

The United States Government made an attempt to provide a national prevalence rate of collating the statistics produced by the designated authorities to which mandatory reports are made. Subsequent research has shown that reports are not always made and there is now good reason to believe that basing a prevalence rate on reported cases will always underestimate the extent of the problem. This is particularly the case in Britain, where reporting is not mandatory and professionals give priority to the obligation to maintain the client's right to confidentiality.

In Great Britain, attempts have been made to establish a national prevalence rate directly, by sample survey of adults, rather than by inference from particular populations or reported cases. Two surveys have been commissioned recently for television companies: in both cases, the consultants were Doctors Baker and Duncan. The findings of the first were published in 1986.[7] In that study, carried out for Channel Four Television, a prevalence rate of 12 per cent for girls and 8 per cent for boys was established. The second survey, for the BBC programme *Childwatch*,[3] yielded an overall rate of 3 per cent, but so few incidents concerning boys were reported that separate rates for boys and girls could not be calculated.

Both surveys asked adults for their childhood experiences and there was evidence of considerable under-reporting. In the Channel Four survey, nearly 13 per cent of respondents refused to answer the questions. In the BBC survey, the interviewers were asked to note when respondents were, in their opinion, concealing an experience of sexual abuse; nearly 4 per cent of the sample were marked in this way. This was more than the number who actually reported having been abused. In addition, 11 per cent of the sample reported having known of a child who was sexually abused. Nash and West[2] compare various American surveys which seem to confirm their rate of between 17 per cent and 25 per cent of women affected. Given all these figures, a 10 per cent prevalence rate for sexual abuse involving physical contact is quite likely.

While the British surveys differed from all other prevalence studies in using a sample designed to be representative of the whole population, they still suffered from serious limitations. Surveys of adults cannot give a current incidence or prevalence rate of the sexual abuse of children, since each individual is reporting on the past. In addition, a measure of under-reporting was built into the design of the survey; the units of the survey were individuals and only one in each house was given the questionnaire. Clinical studies and the details of reported cases show that in a considerable proportion of cases more than one child is abused by the same person, often without the knowledge of the other victims. To trace and interview all the siblings and friends of victims would inevitably have increased the costs of the survey, which would probably have been unacceptable to commercial organisations.

There is evidence that the methods of obtaining information influence the reporting rate. Nash and West[2] circulated questionnaires and then interviewed a number of respondents. Of the abuse that was reported only 6 per cent was discovered at interview; had all respondents to the questionnaire been interviewed, the figure might well have been higher. Russell's San Francisco survey[6] is outstanding for the care taken in choosing and training interviewers; the prevalence rate uncovered was notably higher and almost certainly more accurate than other surveys.

Patterns of sexual abuse

The proportion of children abused within their own homes or outside it is greatly affected by the definition of abuse used and there is controversy over conclusions. The public are deeply reluctant to accept that children may be at risk from their own parents. Finkelhor[4] reports a study of Boston parents which demonstrated that, despite their knowledge about the frequency with which children are abused in their own homes, or by adults they know and trust, respondents persisted in identifying strangers as the main source of sexual threat to children. Baker and Duncan[7] reported that 'strangers' were responsible for 51 per cent of sexual abuse but their later, BBC, survey,[3] using a narrower definition, produced a fraction of that figure for abuse by strangers (16 per cent). Studies of reported cases show a high figure of intra-familial abuse: my own study[8] showed twice as many children abused in their own homes as by outsiders. Abuse by strangers is characteristically limited to few episodes, usually of a milder nature.[2] Baker and Duncan report that girls were slightly more likely to have a single experience and that such experiences were significantly likely to involve strangers; they add that 'exhibitionism probably accounted for a large proportion of such experiences'.[7] Such evidence as we have suggests that serious sexual abuse of children is perpetrated either by members of their own households or by close relatives outside it, although there are rare incidents of the rape of children by strangers.

The sexual abuse of children differs from physical abuse in that it is evenly distributed by region and occupational class.[7] The unpublished results of the BBC survey confirm this finding. Gorry[5] shows that the metropolitan areas of England and Wales have a higher figure of reports of incest but he attributes this to their larger populations; his figures show no great regional variation. No research has yet been undertaken in this country to determine prevalence in cultural or ethnic subgroups compared with the majority. Figures collected by the *American Humane Association national reporting study*[9] show no association between sexual abuse and ethnic origin or class, except for the finding that abusing fathers are less likely to be black. Abusing mothers are more likely than fathers to be black but are still in the minority. Finkelhor's study of university students in the eastern United States[4] does show an apparent association between a rural upbringing and sexual abuse but the numbers are so small as to be statistically dubious. Lukianowicz's study of Irish psychiatric patients,[10] which suggests that incest is a sub-cultural phenomenon, is methodologically flawed and cannot be accepted as it stands.

Figures of reported sexual abuse of children do show a bias towards the lower end of the social scale and some authorities have associated the sexual abuse of children with social disadvantage. However, the evidence suggests that this is probably the result of the manner of disclosure. Gorry[5] reports that incest may come to light when the police are investigating other matters and publishes figures derived from the Incest Crisis Line which show the preponderance of victims of the professional classes among their clients. The BBC survey figures[3] indicate that working-class children have a slightly higher tendency to report abuse than children from other occupational classes. An American study[11] concluded that families where father/daughter incest occurred were predominantly middle class. Research is needed to substantiate the hypothesis, widely accepted by those dealing with the sexual abuse of children, that the extent of sexual abuse among the more advantaged is being effectively concealed.

Discussions of the problem often assume that it concerns male abusers and female victims. Girls do appear as victims in greater numbers than boys; Baker and Duncan[7] report percentages of 12 and 8 respectively. Only very small numbers of men revealed their childhood abuse to interviewers for the BBC survey.[3] However, experience in the United States seems to suggest that, as public awareness has grown, more men are prepared to speak. Finkelhor[4] summarises the American research on boys, and concludes that the pattern of their sexual abuse differed from that of girls. He distinguishes between cases where boys and girls are abused by the same person and those where a boy seemed to be the only victim. Lone male victims were much more likely than lone girls to be victimised by a young adult who was not a family member and to suffer this at a very early age. My study[8] of reported cases indicates a high proportion of boy victims in cases where several children were sexually abused. The subject of male victims has been virtually ignored in Great Britain, and many of the hypotheses put foward by Finkelhor remain to be tested, but it seems likely that research will show some overlap in the cases

involving boys and girls but substantially different patterns otherwise.

Clinical findings and survey material support the conclusion that, of all relatives, both boys and girls are most likely to be abused by a father or stepfather, although it should be noted that the most recent national survey showed a higher percentage of victims of brothers than of stepfathers. Some reports do not distinguish between the father and stepfather, referring instead to father-figures. Where the distinction is made, it appears that the proportion of step-fathers among perpetrators of sexual abuse is greater than their presence in the general population would suggest. There has been no research to determine whether this is merely the result of victims being more willing to report a step-father or whether the type of relationship really is a factor. Finkelhor[4] reviewed the evidence in the United States and concluded that the loss of a father makes children particularly vulnerable to sexual abuse, rather than that stepfathers were particularly prone to be abusers. My study[8] revealed little difference in the kinds of abuse suffered by children from stepfathers or fathers but offered some support for the hypothesis that girls more readily report a stepfather. More research is needed on this point, although the fact that a large number of the perpetrators of abuse are fathers of the victims would seem to indicate that the so-called incest taboo fails to inhibit many men.

Incest between brother and sister (sibling incest) is a neglected aspect of the sexual abuse of children. It is widely considered to be less serious than sexual relations between parent and child. Gorry[7] records that the approach taken by the Director of Public Prosecutions was not to institute proceedings in cases of sibling incest, unless the offence continued after an initial intervention by the authorities. There are several studies which record that siblings are treated comparatively leniently by the courts. Victims report more cases of sibling incest and sexual abuse by a brother than appear in the records, whether of the police or other agencies. Such behaviour may involve the use of force on the victim, contrary to the general view of such behaviour as consensual, but very little is known about the sexual behaviour of children.

An indication that sibling incest may be the con-sequence of parental sexual behaviour was suggested by my study;[8] this conclusion receives support from Smith and Israel's recent study of 25 cases of sibling incest in the United States:[12] in just over half of the cases the abusing sibling had previously been abused by an adult and, in nearly a third, father/daughter incest had preceded the sibling incest.

Survey and clinical material both indicate that children may be sexually abused at an early age. Mrazek, Lynch and Bentovim's postal survey[1] found that 14 per cent of their female patients known to have been abused were five years old or younger; the boys were older; a sizeable proportion were between six and 10. Baker and Duncan[7] report 48 per cent of women abused in childhood who said that they were under 10 at the time but only 27 per cent of the men were as young. Descriptions of clinical cases demonstrate that during treatment victims may remember incidents earlier than the date initially reported as the time the abuse began. Some reports which show a relatively late age of abuse are actually reporting the ages of children at the time abuse was disclosed, which may be several years after it started. Both survey and clinical material show that abuse may persist over considerable periods of time.

There is virtually no research on offenders. They are known to be predominantly male, although a few women are reported, particularly in retrospective surveys. Gibbens, Soothill and Way,[13] in their study of convicted perpetrators of incest, contrast the patterns of criminal behaviour which appear to distinguish those guilty of paternal incest from those convicted of sibling incest. The former had few convictions, both prior to the incident and after they were released, although the incidence of reconviction rose with the passage of time after the date of release. One man, acquitted of incest with his daughter, was convicted 12 years later of the same offence, but with his granddaughter. Some offenders abuse all or most of the children in the household; others appear to choose only one child, usually a girl, but the reason for the different patterns has not been established. Offenders against their siblings have more previous convictions, mostly against property, although some are violent; their subsequent convictions are frequent and the pattern seems to show emotional disturbance. An obvious hypothesis to account for this delinquency would be that it related to antecedent parental behaviour.[8] [12]

The nature of abuse

Clinical reports and accounts of childhood experiences as well as studies of cases in treatment give details of the variety of sexually abusive experiences that may be suffered by children. In many cases there is a progressive course of events, starting with touching and fondling, or exhibitionism, going on to masturbation and then intercourse; anal, oral and vaginal. Of Baker and Duncan's subjects, 5 per cent reported having been subjected to intercourse;[7] the proportion in Nash

and West's survey[2] was 2–3 per cent with an additional 4 per cent having been subject to attempted intercourse. There is insufficient research on the question to be able to suggest factors which prevent the escalation of abuse. It has been suggested that girls who have been victimised at home are at risk of further abuse by others and there is evidence in some surveys to support this.

Consequences of sexual abuse

There is a relatively large literature discussing both long- and short-term effects of sexual abuse in childhood. Mrazek et al[1] point out that most of it is based on material of extremely limited validity. Reports of short-term effects include a variety of emotional and behavioural disturbances and, in the long-term, problems in sexual adjustment, low self-esteem and parenting failures seem the most common. Studies claiming no ill-effects are in a small minority and may even document the pathological consequences that they claim are minimal.[10] Many are quoted in discussions out of context or are generalised without justification. Studies using adult subjects indicate the likelihood of long-term maladjustment but these are mostly based on self-reports rather than psychological testing and do not use controls. Nash and West's study[2] uses sounder methodology: it compares the self-reports of 'abused' and 'non-abused' women from the same sample, concluding that the abused show more frequent signs of maladjustment and general unhappiness than the non-abused. However, six years after Mrazek's critical discussion,[15] the investigation of the effects of sexual abuse in childhood has still not been placed on a sound research footing. What is needed is good epidemiology and some long-term studies of cohorts of children.

Studies of professionals

A number of studies of the work of professional agencies involved in dealing with the sexual abuse of children have been published. Furniss' detailed study of three cases[16] sets out the conflict which may develop between adults with different attitudes and different professional or personal aims. Eisenberg, Owens and Dewey[17] studied health professionals, showing that they underestimated the extent of the problem and that a small percentage even considered the child responsible. Gorry[5] indicates a low rate of referrals from the police to the social services and makes clear that their main aim is to secure convictions; in doing so they must take as their main consideration, not whether an allegation is true or not, but whether the evidence is sufficient to stand up in court. This approach contrasts sharply with that of agencies whose remit is to deal with the social and human problems involved. Finkelhor[4] has demonstrated how, in the United States, conflict between professionals in the criminal justice field and in the social services can derive from their different perceptions and institutional commitments. Other studies in the United States have concluded that attitudes may vary according to gender, but the authors of the study of British professionals recorded that they only found this to be true where estimations of the seriousness of the offence were concerned. Women were much more likely than men to perceive the sexual abuse of children as a serious problem.

Conclusions

Few of the ideas held by members of the general public about the sexual abuse of children are supported by detailed investigation. Nevertheless, some patterns can be established. The rape of a child by a stranger is the rarest form of this offence. Children are most at risk from those living with them, related to them or whom they know. Children rarely lie about having been abused; on the contrary they are rather easily prevailed upon to keep silent and are often not believed when they try to get help. The victims are not newly nubile girls but pre-pubertal children. Boys as well as girls may be abused, sometimes by the same person. Offenders are not 'dirty old men' hanging about near schools, nor criminals, alcoholics or mentally handicapped people, but may be respectable fathers and stepfathers. On the other hand there are many questions still unanswered. Definitions of 'sexual abuse' vary but the major obstacle to research is the secrecy with which events of this nature are surrounded. It seems unlikely that we shall ever know whether children are more often sexually abused now than they were in the past. Much more research needs to be done on the antecedents and consequences of sexual abuse, on possible connections with child pornography and on the offenders as well as the victims.

Summary

Research on this subject shows that there are many public misconceptions about the problems. Policy discussions and public debate also make use of American research, uncritically, and without due consideration of whether it applies in this country. Whilst research on the topic in Great Britain is limited in scope, the findings make an interesting contribution to the current controversies.

The secrecy associated with child sexual abuse is deep-seated. Children may be subjected to a variety of pressures, including threats of violence and death, to prevent their revealing the abuse. Perpetrators often deny having been abusive and may be supported by their spouses in doing so. In some cases they are prepared to commit perjury rather than accept responsibility for their actions. Children, on the contrary, rarely lie about being sexually abused, although they may deny abuse that has happened, to maintain the family secret. Thus only a proportion of cases are disclosed to any authority; it is not likely that they are representative of all cases.

The extent of sexual abuse varies with the definition of the term. For behaviour involving physical contact it is probably 10 per cent of the population. The majority of such cases involve male members of the child's own household or close male kin.

Most public stereotypes of the offence are not supported by research findings. There appears to be no class, regional or ethnic bias in the distribution of sexual offences against children. Little more is known about perpetrators except that they are almost always male. Female offenders only occur in very small numbers. Characteristics such as alcoholism, criminality or unemployment may be attributed to offenders but without any comparison with the prevalence of such factors in the general population.

The sexual abuse of boys and girls seems to show rather different patterns. It is probable that girls are abused more often than boys, but there is no research on male victims of sexual abuse in childhood. Some children of both sexes are abused at a very early age and the majority of victims are pre-pubertal.

While there is a great deal written about the effects of sexual abuse on children, much less is based on sound research. Retrospective studies of adults indicate the likelihood of long-term damage. Some research suggests that victims of abuse are at risk of abusing their own children or are unable to protect them from being abused.

Studies of professionals involved in work with cases of the sexual abuse of children show their opinions differing according to the nature of their institutional involvement; such studies also demonstrate the potential for conflict between professionals of different organisations.

References

1 Mrazek, P B, Lynch M and Bentovim A 'Recognition of child sexual abuse in the United Kingdom' in Mrazek P B and Kemp C H (eds) *Sexually abused children and their families* Pergamon, 1981.

2 Nash C L and West D J 'Sexual molestation of young girls' in West D J (ed) *Sexual victimisation* Gower Press, 1985.

3 BBC survey for *Childwatch*, unpublished.

4 Finkelhor D *Child sexual abuse: new theory and research* Collier Macmillan, 1984.

5 Gorry P J 'Incest: the offence and police investigation' unpublished M Phil Thesis in Criminology, University of Cambridge, 1986.

6 Russell D E H *The secret trauma: incest in the lives of girls and women* New York: Basic Books, 1986.

7 Baker A and Duncan S 'Child sexual abuse: a study of prevalence in Great Britain' *Child Abuse and Neglect* 9, 1986.

8 La Fontaine J S 'A sociological study of cases of child sexual abuse in Britain' ESRC end of award report no. G0023 2244, 1987.

9 American Humane Association 'American Humane Association national reporting study' Denver, Colorado, 1978.

10 Lukianowicz N 'Incest 1 – Paternal incest: 2 – Other types of incest' *Brit J Psychiat* 120, 1972.

11 Browne L and Holder W 'The nature and extent of child abuse in contemporary American society' in Holder W (ed) *Sexual abuse of children* American Humane Association, Denver, Colorado, 1980.

12 Smith H and Israel E 'Siblings incest: the study of the dynamics of 25 cases' *Child Abuse and Neglect* 11 (1), 1987.

13 Gibbens T C W, Soothill K I and Way C K 'Sibling and parent-child incest offenders: a long term follow-up' *Brit J Criminol* 18 (1), 1978.

14 Yurokoglu A and Kemph J P 'Children not severely damaged by incest with the parent' *J Amer Acad Child Psychiat* 5, 1966.

15 Mrazek P B 'The effects of child sexual abuse: methodological considerations' in Mrazek P B and Kemp C H (eds) *Sexually abused children and their families* Pergamon, 1981.

16 Furniss T 'Family process in the treatment of intrafamilial sexual abuse' in *J Fam Ther* 5 (4), 1983.

17 Eisenberg N, Owens R G and Dewey M E 'Attitudes of health professionals to child sexual abuse and incest' *Child Abuse and Neglect* 11 (1), 1987.

Child sexual abuse: the power of intrusion

Gerrilyn Smith

The *context* of work in child sexual abuse has an effect on the work that we can do. In my experience the degree of overlap between those who use child guidance clinics, rape crisis centres and social services departments is quite small.

Referrals for sexual abuse to child guidance clinics more often involve an abuser who is outside the immediate nuclear family. These range from strangers to more distant relatives like uncles or grandfathers. Social services departments, on the other hand, tend to deal with intrafamilial abuse: that is to say, the abuser and the child live in the same home. Rape crisis centres are often used by those who would not contact 'official' agencies or who may have already done so and not been satisfied with the service they have received.

Because my observations are based on my experiences within these different working contexts, the conclusions may be more a reflection of passing time and an increased awareness regarding sexual abuse generally. Nonetheless, I was always struck by the distance and anonymity a telephone line allows. This appeals to some girls and young women who might not otherwise speak out. A balance seemed to be struck by the power of emotions on the one hand, and the actual physical distance of the caller on the other. Finding the right distance to do the work generated by child sexual abuse is crucial.

In the vast majority of cases, my colleagues and I are working with allegations that remain unproven in law. We also work primarily with adolescents, which is considerably different from working with younger children. We have had to learn to deliver a service often in the absence of confessions and convictions.

My subject matter will be in two parts: first, the definition and recognition of child sexual abuse; and second, treatment and the role of the alternative family. There are several assumptions I will make.

There is no one way of dealing with sexual abuse. It is a very complex subject. I will often use the generic 'she' in this paper when referring to children who have been abused and the generic 'he' when referring to abusers. Women do sexually abuse children but it is overwhelmingly males who abuse both girl and boy children.

The issue of blood relations obscures what is at the root of all child sexual abuse: the betrayal of trust and the abuse of power to achieve personal gratification.[1] None of us has been trained for equal relationships. All of us have been indoctrinated into what I will call a psychology of subordination and domination. Consequently the vast majority of us will have abused power but not necessarily by using sex as the means to do it.

I do not subscribe to the theory that certain types of families sexually abuse their children, or that sexual abuse is a symptom of deeper family problems. I believe sexual abuse could happen in any family. All families must establish limits and boundaries. All families must teach their members about sexuality, relationships and respect. Findings on family type are based on research carried out after it is known abuse has occurred. These studies are not predictive. We cannot tell beforehand who will or will not abuse their children. We also do not have access to those parents who were sexually abused as children and then go on successfully to protect their own children.

As long as we live in a society in which the right of every individual to say 'no' is not respected, we will always have sexual abuse. Sexual abuse is a form of oppression by the powerful of the powerless. Children do not have a place in the public debate. They rely on us, as adults, to put across their point of view.

Although I will be using the term child sexual abuse, I include within it incest. Incest has a very specific meaning within the law. It is possible to see and understand sexual abuse as a continuum from a single abusive incident to continuous assaults. It is also important to recognise the range of potential abusers, from strangers to acquaintances to fathers.

In order to recognise sexual abuse, we need to know what it is. Unfortunately, there are many myths that surround sexual abuse. These beliefs, very firmly held, often make it more difficult for us to recognise sexual abuse.

Definitions

The definitions I am going to supply are not legal ones. I would like to urge workers to recognise the difference between what is required by law to prove sexual abuse and what is required by counsellors. The following definition is very graphic and spells out exactly what sexual abuse involves. This is necessary because people frequently concentrate on sexual intercourse as the only form of abuse.

'Sexual assault means the forcing of sexual contact. This can involve handling the child's genitals or requests for sexual handling by an older child or adult. Sometimes, the contact is oral sex. Sexual contact includes attempts at penetration of the vagina or anus. Sometimes actual penetration occurs. It can involve penetration by penis, but also fingers and objects can be used. Some assaults involve no physical contact. A child may be forced to look at the genitals of an older child or an adult,

This article first appeared in *Adoption & Fostering* 10 3, 1986.

forced to watch adults having sex, forced to perform sexual acts in front of an adult(s), forced to undress or otherwise expose themselves.'[2] I would add 'spied on and photographed in private personal situations'. It is important to know this detail because you must be prepared for what a child or young person might reveal to you. It will help you to understand how difficult this is to talk about.

When we talk of force we mean: taking advantage of someone who is younger; bribery; threats of harming the child or their family; threats of what will happen to the abuser; withdrawal of affection, love, attention; sometimes actual physical force is used but the threat of it is implicit. These types of force are frequently used in combination.[3]

We must recognise the common misconceptions about sexual abuse. By knowing what it is and how it happens you will be better prepared to support both children and their carers. You will also be more able to spot some of the signs that abuse is or has been occurring. So what is sexual assault?

What we fear[4]	What is more likely
A dangerous, weird stranger	A person they know (85% of the time)
Violent attack	Bribery and threats, rather than extreme physical force
Out of the blue, surprises	A situation that develops gradually over a period of time
Isolated extreme incident	Frequent incidents taking many forms

Recognising what sexual abuse is and how it happens, or the form it can take, is an absolute prerequisite in this type of work. How can you help someone speak the unspeakable when it remains unimaginable for you?

Unassailed these misconceptions continue to protect abusers and leave children at risk. We, as professionals, often perpetuate them in reports and letters that we write. For example, here is an excerpt from a professional's letter: 'In my experience, children subject to sexual assault, even of a rather violent nature, are rarely emotionally affected by this. Of course if subjected to repeated assaults or interference over a prolonged period of time they are more likely to become emotionally disturbed.' It indicates a clear misunderstanding of child sexual abuse. The child involved in this case was a young boy, six years old, whose father was eventually convicted of buggering his son. The professional's letter was written after the conviction. The professional was also requested to assess the likelihood of sexual abuse occurring, a request often made of professionals. To this he responds: '. . . it seems that there is little real evidence that the father is making sexual advances to this child, the mother being just as likely a culprit.'

Here the child's allegations were corroborated by medical evidence and a confession.

The mother's culpability is raised and reinforced by additional comments in the GP's report, which includes this 'fact': 'There has been no sexual intercourse between marriage partners since the wedding night 17 years ago when an unsuccessful attempt resulted in Mr X being afraid to touch his wife again.'

This couple have a six-year-old child. Yet a picture is emerging where deprivation of conjugal rights is an excuse for buggering a six-year-old child.

The notion of collusion abounds in theories of child sexual abuse. In order to collude, one has knowingly to conspire to commit a crime. One cannot unconsciously collude, something of which mothers are often accused. One can be negligent or fail to protect. And in this respect, we as professionals must also recognise and accept our responsibilities.

Other commonly held beliefs that are not borne out by my experience are:

1. Children lie about sexual abuse
In considering this we need to ask ourselves the following questions:
i) Why would children lie?
ii) Why do we as adults find it hard to believe?
iii) How can children tell us about sexual abuse?

2. Children are seductive and enjoy the experience
i) Can a child bear the responsibility of an adult's action?
ii) Is seduction in the eye of the beholder?
iii) The helping profession's psychoanalytic past rears its head. The idea of infant sexuality can be used to reapportion blame for sexual abuse of children (Lolita).
iv) The healthy need for physical contact and love that all children have is misconstrued and exploited.

3. Men who sexually abuse children are paedophiles or have a sexual interest in children
Although this is true in some cases, it denies the experience of women and girls who are abused by brothers, whose fathers wait until they are pubescent, and who continue to abuse them into their adult lives.

Case example
The following referral is an example that illustrates

some of these misconceptions in operation.

An eight-year-old girl is referred to a child guidance clinic by her mother. The referral form asks the parents to fill in some questions. In answer to the question 'How do you see the problem?' the mother writes: 'The child has a preoccupation about sex, leading to accusations against her stepfather; also problems arising from the divorce.' In answer to the question 'How does the child see it?' the mother writes: 'She says the accusations are true and sees no wrong in the implications or seriousness of the matter. She is disgusted by the exposure of the female body on TV: for example, dancers, scantily clad. She does not like anyone to see her undressed except her mother . . . which does not tie in with her accusations.' And in answer to the question 'How do you think this department can help?' the mother writes 'She needs to see a qualified person before going to visit her real father. Unless the situation is brought under control she will permanently develop an inherent dislike of men.'

Contained within this referral we have good examples of myths in operation. First and foremost we have the lying. This is referred to as 'accusations the child thinks are true'. We also have the notion that children are seductive. The mother believes that the child's preoccupation with sex is what leads to the accusations. There is no understanding that the preoccupation may be an attempt on the child's part to understand what has already happened to her. We also have the idea that children enjoy the experience. This is intimated by the mother's confusion regarding the child's fear of getting undressed in front of anyone. The mother seems to think that the child, from her accusations, should enjoy getting undressed. It is clear that the adult is worried about the seriousness and implications of the accusations, and this she projects onto her child. For if the accusations are true then the mother must act. Here the mother can only ask for help with the child's 'lying'.

It would be very easy in this example to see this mother as colluding. However, mothers are a very convenient scapegoat. We need to ask ourselves who else may know about this and does not act. Families contain more people than just mothers. There are brothers, sisters, aunts, uncles, grandparents. There are even neighbours. There are teachers, health visitors and doctors.

Who can mothers go to? What do they get advised when they do go? A large number of calls at rape crisis centres are from mothers ringing because of their concerns. In this particular incident we, the child guidance clinic, become responsible, as we have reason to believe the child is being sexually abused. The mother, by referring to us, is asking for help.

Two other characteristics were also present in this referral. First, the reaction that children who have been sexually abused need to be seen by a qualified person. In my experience this is very common. I often feel that it conveys to a child that what has happened to her or him is so terrible and awful that no one can talk about it except this strange person. In working with families where children have been sexually abused by members outside the immediate nuclear family, I have usually worked with the parents rather than directly with the child. In doing this, I have tried to support the parents so that they in turn can support their child.

It is in the context of everyday living that the child's worries, fears, doubts and anxieties come out, not in the context of an hour a week within a therapy session. I feel the former is more healthy and I question whether children can knowingly consent to enter therapy. In keeping with this line of reasoning, foster families, with support, could undertake work that would be very effective.

The second characteristic present in the case example is what I call the seeding of an alternative interpretation or explanation of the child's behaviour. Here it was the divorce. It would be very easy for me, as a psychologist, to grab onto the issue of divorce, given it is something I feel relatively confident to deal with. However, it is important that we are not tempted to spend time and energy following up the second alternative without exploring the first, most obvious, reason for the child's disturbance, the sexual abuse.

Treatment

The importance of conveying belief to a child or young person who tells you of her or his experience of sexual abuse cannot be underestimated. These children may ask numerous times if you believe them. The following are some of the basic points that I think should be made clear to anyone who has been sexually abused:

– a belief in their account
– the abuser was wrong and knew what he was doing was wrong
– what happened was not their fault
– the angry feelings that may be apparent are directed at the abuser and not the child. This is very important for often young children pick up a parent's immediate sense of rage at which has happened and mistakenly believe that the rage is directed towards them rather than towards the perpetrator
– you are glad the child has come to tell you and it

was the right thing to do.

There are a large number of preventive programmes being marketed here in the UK. You can spend a whole day at the Health Education Council viewing videos on preventing child sexual abuse. There are favourable and unfavourable aspects of each programme. Which you will prefer will be a matter of personal taste but all these programmes emphasise a child's right to say 'no'. This emphasis shifts the responsibility to protect oneself onto the child. It is a sad indictment of adults that this is necessary. None of the programmes works towards preventing children from becoming abusers.

Speaking out about sexual abuse in the family frequently involves a loyalty conflict. In the situation of young black women, it also involves the betrayal or perceived disloyalty to the black community as a whole. There is a fear (and it must be emphasised that this fear is founded in the experience of black people) that revelation of sexual abuse within the black community will possibly be used to feed the racist assumptions of white people and lead to personal ostracism from that community. I have heard variations on the following in my work:
– a natural expectation that black men are both physically and sexually violent
– single parent families are predisposed to sexual abuse occurring, with abusers coming in the form of multiple boyfriends
– sexual abuse is culturally defined and not seen as such in some cultures, especially primitive ones.

If the young woman's telling involves the authorities, it often means bringing predominantly white authorities, such as the police and social services, into black family life. This is something from which black families may have protected themselves.

Gender is important in this kind of work. So too is race. This is not to say that white workers cannot work with black families. We need not only to name our differences but also to recognise the power imbalances these variables, sex and race, bring into play, regardless of the actual circumstances.

In working with young black women or families, I always state there may be things they feel unable to discuss with me because I am a white woman. There are enough misconceptions surrounding child sexual abuse for any young person to deal with, let alone taking on board the ignorance, or worse, racist ideas of supposed helpers about black people and black family life.

It is important to recognise that it is almost impossible to choose to live outside family life. Single people, for instance, are often perceived as between families. To choose not to have a family is

not on offer to many children. This is less true for adolescents.

Foster families

The first consideration, with regard to alternative families, is whether or not foster parents know before placement if a child has been sexually abused. Unfortunately, I think in only a small minority of instances will this be the case. In my experience, it is often only after the abuse has stopped and/or the possibility of being returned to the abuser removed, that a child will begin to talk about her or his experiences. Maybe that distance and security are needed to examine something so painful.

Many children will reveal for the first time that they were abused sexually after being in a placement for a while. It may be that their behaviour suggested this may be the case but the actual articulating of it happens later.

Although adolescents require quite different parenting from younger children, sometimes that sixteen-year-old has a raging eight-year-old inside. You may find yourself comforting that child, so even teenage placement projects could use the approaches developed for younger children as part of their training.

What are some of the problems experienced when placing a child or young person we know to have been sexually abused in an alternative family? From my experience there seems to be a reluctance on the part of foster families to take in a child or young person known to have been sexually abused. This is often based on ignorance and/or lack of support about what it would entail.

There is the fear of introducing potentially sexually explosive material into 'normal' family life. Foster families need help with this. How has sexuality been discussed in their families? What, if any, preventive work have they done with their own children? How much should they tell their own children about the foster child's experience? If sexually explicit behaviour occurs, how will the foster parents and other family members deal with it constructively and sensitively?

In addition, foster parents often raise their anxiety about future allegations being made about members of their families. This issue needs to be discussed fully. How can a family minimise the risk of this occurring? Reassurances need to be made that in a believing and accepting atmosphere a child or young person will not add to their original allegations. As workers, we need to be prepared to consider that a child may be telling the truth when accusing a member of the foster family of sexual abuse.

Ignoring the 'sexualised' behaviour of an abused child (and not all sexually abused children demonstrate such behaviour) is a recipe for disaster. We need to recognise that the behaviour is a consequence of the abuse. The child has been sexualised by the abuser. Other adults must de-sexualise her. Young children learn to behave sexually to get their needs met. They learn love is contingent upon sexual favours.

A therapeutic placement would be one in which the child was taught that it is not necessary to use her body sexually to get her needs for love, affection and attention met. It would work towards strengthening her existing coping mechanisms and developing new ones. An ideal placement must prevent further abuse and attempt, with support, to resolve the effects of past abuse.

References

1 Incest Survivors Campaign provide a similar definition: 'Sexual molestation of a child by any person that the child sees as a figure of trust or authority. The question of blood relationship can be seen as a red herring which obscures the central issue: the irresponsible sexual exploitation of children's ignorance, trust and obedience'.

2 Adams Caren and Fay Jennifer, *No more secrets: protecting your child from sexual assault* Impact Publishers, 1981.

3 See 2 above.

4 See 2 above.

3 Child sexual abuse and race issues

Maria Mars

The aim of this chapter is to explore some of the difficulties experienced by black children who have been sexually abused. It is argued that institutionalised racism and sexism in our society affect not only the ways in which social services, the police and other agencies respond to the disclosure of abuse, but also the ways in which the family involved responds.

Child sexual abuse occurs right across the social spectrum regardless of class, gender, race and culture. It is a crime committed mainly by men against children (mainly girls) of all ages. Child sexual abuse is viewed as a violation and betrayal of the child's love and trust.

In this chapter the discussion will focus on the following:
– misconceptions about child sexual abuse/assault
– race issues and child sexual abuse
– professional issues; training and policy recommendations

Misconceptions about child sexual abuse/assault

It is essential to know what sexual abuse is and to try to understand how it starts, what it involves and how it continues, so that we can recognise and deal effectively with suspected or confirmed cases.

Child sexual abuse is a silent crime. It occurs in secret, generally within the privacy of the family. Recent figures indicate that one in 10 children have been sexually abused at one time or another. In most cases abusers are members of the family or individuals known and trusted by the family. This is contrary to popular belief that abusers are strangers with paedophile tendencies.

It is often suggested that child sexual abuse is an isolated extreme incident and that abusers suffer from a form of psychopathology. Clinical evidence shows that sexual abuse of the child does not happen out of the blue, but that it is often premeditated and carefully planned. Abusers tend to use the intimate knowledge they have of their victims and to employ the most effective method of continuing the abuse. This may take the form of threats, rejection, bribery or actual physical violence.

It has been suggested that children lie and fantasise about sexual abuse. In fact, the evidence shows that children rarely lie about it – and, when they do, it is to say it has not happened when it has. Another belief is that sexual abuse, particularly with siblings, is not serious. However, those of us who work with victims of abuse know that the experience has a damaging effect on the child's self-esteem, mental health, and on his or her ability to form meaningful sexual relationships, regardless of who the perpetrator was.

Childhood is a vulnerable time in the development of sexuality. Children are physically and psychologically unprepared for sexual stimulation:

Where the chances of harming a child's normal development are concerned, it [sexual abuse] ranks higher than abandonment, neglect, physical maltreatment or any other form of abuse. It would be a total mistake to underrate the implication or frequency of its actual occurrence. (Anna Freud, 1981, quoted in The CIBA Foundation's *Child sexual abuse within the family* Tavistock, 1984.)

Child sexual abuse is rooted in centuries of sexual inequality and male domination, and there is no one solution to the problem. Nevertheless we must create a climate in which professionals and the general public are encouraged to recognise the sexual abuse of children and to respond in a way that will ensure the protection and safety of the child, regardless of race, gender or class.

Race and child sexual abuse

The issue of child sexual abuse as it relates to the black communities should not be viewed in isolation, but it is crucial for professionals and others involved in child protection work to be aware that there are specific difficulties experienced by black children who have been or are being sexually abused. It can be argued that these arise as a result of institutionalised racism, which serves to compound the impact of child sexual abuse on the black child. Many black children are aware that black people's presence in Britain is unwelcome and is viewed with hostility and violence. Many black families have had negative – even bitter – experiences with social services, the police and the education service. It follows that in an attempt to protect black family life, the black communities have built barriers around themselves.

For the black child who is being sexually abused within his or her own family, to tell means: making themselves more vulnerable; inviting social services and police involvement; betraying and letting down their family and community; and providing a further basis for reinforcing racist stereotypes of black communities. These factors only serve to further silence the child.

Case examples

Adult survivor – 30 years old
Meg was sexually abused by her father from the age

of 11 to 15. She did not tell her mother because she felt she would not be believed; and decided not to tell her teachers, who were all white, because they would not understand black family life and already held racist views of black people. When she was 27 years old Meg eventually told her mother, who then begged her not to tell anyone, because it would bring 'shame' on the family name.

Adult survivor – 22 years old
Pam was sexually abused by her half-brother (six years older) from the age of eight to 15. She became pregnant at 15. She tried to tell her mother, who did not believe her. Pam also tried to tell her social worker but no one wanted to know. She became quiet and withdrawn and did not want to speak to anyone. Pam's teachers became concerned and she was sent to see a psychiatrist. Family meetings were held but the family did not talk. Pam could not tell the psychiatrist, who was a white man, and there were no black workers to talk to. Eventually she went to the police station and reported what was happening. The police surgeon (a white man) told her she was two months pregnant and she was received into care.

Pam's family accused her of betraying them to 'Babylon' (meaning the police) and have never forgiven her. When she was seven months pregnant she suffered a mental breakdown. Pam felt evil and sinful and that she had betrayed her family.

Attitudes vary to the significance of the race of the professional who attempts to undertake work with the sexually-abused black child and family. It has been pointed out that most white professionals lack awareness of the problems, feelings and outlook of black families, while black clients in their turn doubt the sincerity of the 'helping' white professionals and ask for black professionals to work with them. We may feel that skin colour has such an enormous significance in our society that a black person's condition will be totally different from that of a white citizen.

However, the author supports the view that any white professional who has an understanding of the client's current personality, cultural and social background, the political realities of black existence and an awareness of such issues as the continued survival of black life can work effectively with the black child and family. The gender of the professional can also be highly significant to the child.

The initial contact between the professional and the family is of vital importance and can determine the outcome of the case. A number of factors may limit the professional's understanding of black families:

Racist attitudes
Many white workers evaluate and assess black families by means of a set of assumptions based on racist stereotypes. This adds to the complexity of the assessment process. An anti-racist approach would serve to promote positive communication and help to build a good client/worker relationship.

Language
If there is no common language, the worker will find it impossible to carry out an accurate and satisfactory assessment. Black language (e.g. Jamaican) could be easily misunderstood – words and idioms are usually accompanied by gestures, body motions and voice changes.

Cultural/social background
Religion and class are important variables to be considered during the assessment process: for instance, it is important for the worker to understand what it means to be a Hindu, a Muslim, a Jew or a Rastafarian.

Sometimes professionals find it difficult to know what degree of sexual contact is abusive and what is part of the family's appropriate affectionate contact. It is true that the extent and nature of touching between parents and children varies in different cultures; but when the boundary between the demonstration of affection and sexual stimulation or exploitation is crossed, what occurs can be clearly seen as abusive.

It is necessary to recognise the wide range of languages, religions, and cultures which form the basis of different life-styles and workers must be aware of the institutionalised racism and sexism and their damaging effects. Without such awareness and a strong commitment to an anti-racist and anti-sexist approach, workers will continue to assess black families on stereo-typical racist assumptions.

Some ways forward

The solution to the problem of child sexual abuse lies in family life, education and the raised consciousness of society at large. We must aim to create a climate where workers involved in child protection work have access to training which enables them to recognise and deal effectively with suspected or confirmed child sexual abuse as well as to offer support and adequate care to the child and family, and where families need not be afraid that exposure will necessarily lead to family breakdown with children in care. Removal of the child from the family must be the last resort after all other courses of action have been tried and where there is no one in the child's family (including extended family) or community who can support and protect him or her.

Some professionals are becoming increasingly concerned about removing children from their family homes as there may be inadequate provision of safe places for children in the care of local authorities. It is a disturbing fact that some children experience further sexual abuse whilst in care – in community homes and in foster placements. In addition, because many social services departments are understaffed, a large number of child sexual abuse cases are not being allocated.

Community voluntary organisations are becoming more aware of the need to protect the child as they recognise that social services departments cannot always do this adequately. A 14-year-old black girl who has been in care for the last ten years told me that she did not believe social services could protect her. She was sexually abused by her father and then by two other male carers whilst in care. Realising that social workers could not protect her she had gone back to her community and established links with family friends (in this case, three black women) who have since used their community network to confront her father regarding the sexual assault. Professionals need to develop clear links with community groups and to work closely with families not only when there is a crisis, so that long-term plans can be made to meet the needs of the child.

To counteract the negative views of black people, professionals must take into account the historical experiences of black people and their relationships with statutory agencies – particularly social services and the police. Already there are too many black children in care, simply because many white social workers lack sufficient knowledge and understanding of black family life and have a general tendency to assess black families within a traditional white framework.

Giving workers information about the variety of cultures and languages in the black communities is not enough for, despite the common experiences shared by black groups, black people differ widely both as a result of economic status and to the extent to which they assimilate British/Western values and perspectives.

Workers must guard against racist stereotyping which may influence not only plans for casework with the parents and children but also access for parents and rehabilitation. We have much to gain from building a good client/worker relationship. Every consideration must be given to protecting and ensuring the safety of the child. Community organisations should be encouraged and supported in setting up projects – safe centres for children, free legal services for non-abusing parents, counselling services for women who have been sexually assaulted, etc, etc. All policies, guidelines and procedures on the management of child sexual abuse should reflect a race dimension.

4 Personal and professional issues in child sexual abuse

Gerrilyn Smith

This chapter is a brief introduction to some of the issues, attitudes and feelings that arise in the field of child sexual abuse. Throughout the chapter the assumed form of sexual abuse is intra-familial with father or father-figure as the perpetrator, as this is the most common form of sexual abuse.

Child sexual abuse raises powerful gender issues. It is unfortunately not wholly different from normal experience: it touches on everyday activities and is reflected in everyday life. Child sexual abuse is an extreme form of sexual exploitation. It is typically women and children who are sexually exploited by men. In dealing with child sexual abuse, different issues will arise for men and women.

Many of the questions asked of abused children could be asked of ourselves. What would I do? What would I say? In child sexual abuse work you are essentially alone. You are responsible for the decisions you will make. You may or may not get the support you need or want. The pressures on you to reconstruct the evidence are very high. This essentially lonely position of the worker mirrors that of the child and it is through that parallel that we must draw courage and strength. We as adult men and women must believe in the responsible exercise of authority and strive to demonstrate it in our lives and our work. What that means for us personally and professionally is that we must confront the irresponsible exercise of authority and challenge those powerful others who do so. Sexual exploitation is only one area of abuse. There are many others.

We must develop a heightened sensibility to the pressures a privileged position brings to bear on the less privileged. So we need to recognise the difficulties of working across race, gender and class.

This chapter is divided into three sections: the worker, the child and the family of origin. Conceptual models are referred to throughout the paper with very little commentary regarding their theoretical constructs. A conceptual model might be a social or political framework by which you analyse the phenomenon, or it might be a type of therapeutic intervention such as psychotherapy, behaviour therapy or family therapy. Whatever your perspective you should be clear about the shortcomings and areas of weakness in your approach and strive not to become dogmatic.

As a psychologist, I consider understanding to be a crucial part of my work. Yet in child sexual abuse work I am constantly confronted by things I cannot understand – or perhaps do not wish to. Understanding, however, does not imply acceptance. It is important that you have a position on the moral implications of child sexual abuse for it will affect you personally and professionally as it is uncovered.

Issues for the worker

Child sexual abuse is an extremely stressful area of work. It will tax you personally and professionally. It will challenge some of your most deeply-held assumptions and keep you awake at night worrying over whether you have made the right decisions. To survive working in this field you need a good support network, both personal and professional, as well as a clear conceptual model on which to base your work.

It is important to be clear about what you hope to achieve. There are two guidelines I give to people I am training to enable them to cope with the stress of child sexual abuse work. The first is that you never know *exactly* what happened between the perpetrator and the target of abuse. At best you can offer educated (and, we hope, well-informed) guesswork. To be placed in the position of arbiter of truth is a heavy responsibility. I feel the only way to free yourself from this potentially paralysing position is to recognise that there is never only one truth, merely different perceptions of the same events. As workers you review those events at second- or third-hand, which makes them even more difficult to assess. However, you are still able to offer an opinion as to which is the most probable explanation for the current crisis. Despite differing conceptual models, almost all workers with experience of child sexual abuse agree that children rarely make false allegations. So when a child or young person makes a disclosure of sexual abuse, the onus of disproof should fall on the adult perpetrator. You must use your professional judgement in weighing up the probabilities and offering an opinion.

The second caveat is that you can only stop child sexual abuse if you are *actively* involved. The main task is to try and prevent it from happening again and to pick up the pieces afterwards. Workers cannot be held responsible for the abuse itself despite the media insistence that they are. As professionals involved in child care, you have a responsibility to protect to the best of your ability. Very often the context of child protection work is a backdrop of overworked, overstressed and unprotected workers. We must recognise the irony of giving a group of professionals the responsibility to protect and care for abused children and then leaving them to carry out this work unprotected and uncared for. So it is important to set *achievable* goals.

The first step in coming to terms with personal experience is a recognition of that experience. Once individuals have appraised themselves of a situation, they can begin to deal with it. With child sexual abuse, this is crucial to the recovery process both for the individual and for the family members. We need to recognise that there are still many people who do not accept that child sexual abuse happens with the frequency it does, as well as those who accept that it happens but do not consider it harmful.

Because this experience is also a criminal activity on the part of the perpetrator, it is frequently dealt with in a legalistic framework rather than a thera-peutic one. Interviews are sometimes conducted in an atmosphere of stress and anxiety and questions asked that imply other more benign explanations of the child's statement. In other circumstances, children may be pressurised to make a disclosure. It is extremely difficult to find the balance in diagnostic interviews that can be used in court.

Child sexual abuse is something that touches everybody: consequently, all sorts of people feel perfectly at liberty to comment on the merits of a case. So it is not uncommon that, despite an investigation having been done, other workers involved in the case feel the need to make their own minds up. This feeling of constantly being under scrutiny is very unpleasant. We have to be confident in the assessments we carry out and able to deal with the doubt a positive finding of sexual abuse generates. In my experience, it only takes one expert witness to disprove allegations of sexual abuse but a minimum of two to prove the allegations.

The fear and doubt generated by a positive finding mirrors the fear and doubt a family must feel with the dawning realisation that a major problem exists within it. The professional system, to maintain its integrity and cohesiveness, must operate within high levels of concordance. It must also, at the same time, admit and examine evidence that disputes its own appraisal of the situation. If this is not seen as an accepted part of teamwork, then the opposing explanations can be construed as disbelief and lack of support. In order to facilitate this questioning process, it would be worthwhile to assign someone the specific task of coming up with other explanations for the current pattern of information. For the individual worker this is extremely difficult, as it usually involves another person to bounce ideas off. On the whole, we are not trained to think this way. Life becomes infinitely more complex if we have to choose, from a range of possible explanations, the one that fits best. The widening professional and public debate on child sexual abuse has forced us to do so. It is interesting that this topic is the one that pushes people to think differently.

If part of your conceptualisation of child sexual abuse is the recognition of the irresponsible exercise of authority, you may understand why child sexual abuse would be the issue to promote such a re-examination of our methods of practice. Alice Miller, in her book *Thou shalt not be aware: Society's betrayal of the child*, makes the point that we, as adults, often unconsciously side with other adults when we are confronted with adult wrongdoings perpetrated on children.[1] Any child-centred approach to children's protection is going to compromise the rights and privileges of adults, so we need to be prepared for their reaction to this.

As sexual abuse frequently happens within the context of the family and is perpetrated by a family member, it also challenges assumptions about the sanctity and safety of the family unit. We construct ways of allowing ourselves to continue to support the family unit, despite our knowledge of the brutalities perpetuated in it. The idea of the family as a safe nurturing place is of central importance in most cultures. When a child's family of origin fails to provide that safe nurturing place, we put professional energy into finding that child a 'substitute family'. A family is almost impossible to substitute because it does not just go away when you are not with it. For children and young people who no longer have a place in their family of origin, offering an alternative family helps them to understand that families, contrary to media images, come in many shapes and sizes. They organise differently and there is no single formula for family success. Clearly, more work is needed on what helps to predict the families where sexual abuse might occur. Professionally and legally we should not be dominated by the idea of what is taken as the norm (a mother, a father and children).

Issues for the child

The issues confronting a child who has been (or is being) sexually assaulted are numerous and complex. It is also important to remember that in the normal course of events no child should be confronted with them. For children and young people sexual abuse is something that, because of their dependency on the family, they are forced to learn to live with. This is what Roland Summit referred to as the accommodation syndrome.[2] I think it is profoundly disturbing that the needs of one person (usually male) should dominate the needs of others to such an extent that the others (usually women and children) are expected to accommodate them, even when they are as unreasonable as this.

The social mores of this syndrome are so strong that children recognise it without needing to be told directly about it. In many ways, the issues are already set for children, for they have been put in a position they should not be in and consequently *have* to learn to deal with it. Perhaps the biggest issue is whether or not to tell. Already the focus for the child has shifted from whether or not it should happen. This is not a decision a child can make. In deciding what to do, a child must weigh up many factors. It is relatively easy to generate a list of good reasons not to tell and more difficult to make a list of reasons to tell.[3] Each child weighs up the pros and cons of disclosing. Even recognising at some level that their silence is needed for the sexual abuse to continue, they will often decide that to be abused is the least worst option. In other words they are prepared to sacrifice themselves to the supposed greater good of family unity.

There are clear gender differences in the rate of disclosures. We know that the actual rate of child sexual abuse is difficult to assess, but we suspect that boys are under-represented in figures of incidence and prevalence.[4] In considering why this is so, we need to recognise the very different way families socialise girls and boys. For example, girls are encouraged to ask other people for help, whereas boys are encouraged to figure things out for themselves.

Like girls, boys are most often sexually assaulted by adult men. Consequently boy children are confronted with having to make sense of what seems to be a homosexual assault. Because our society does not promote discussion about homosexuality, it leaves boys who have been sexually assaulted by men (and the same would be true of girls sexually assaulted by women) doubly silenced by the taboos of what our society considers normal. The boy child may feel that an experience of this kind could 'make him a homosexual'. The very language used indicates the homophobic frame of reference. The idea of people being 'made into homosexuals' removes the element of choice or preference in sexual partners. Children who have been sexually assaulted need reassurances that they can make choices in their lives and that past experience does not always dictate further development.

In the girl child, the heterosexual nature of the abuse allows people to assume it is 'more normal' and, in some circumstances, perhaps even understandable (as in step-fathers sexually assaulting teenage step-daughters). Boys are rarely described as promiscuous or provocative, labels frequently used in relation to adolescent girls.

These words, 'promiscuous' or 'provocative', imply a certain degree of responsibility for the abuse. Even the law views the crime differently depending on the age of the girl. Under the age of 13 a girl is considered not to be physically mature enough for intercourse. After 13, incest and unlawful sexual intercourse are still considered crimes but are less serious in terms of sentencing. The onset of puberty is seen to diminish the severity of the abuse and an inferred biological readiness imputes the girl child with a degree of complicity in her abuse.

So we can see how subtly the notion of girls actively participating is interwoven into the understanding of sexual abuse. Boys as sexual predators cause concern only when the object of their sexual attentions is seen as unsuitable, usually younger children and/or other boys. The point has been made elsewhere, but perhaps can be re-stated here, that children who have been repeatedly sexually assaulted become sexualised. They become the sexual objects their abusers have made them into. To give up or throw off the sexual projections of an abuser means confronting the fear that you have no other use or value. Physical attractiveness and sexual desirability are both highly valued in our society. The message then to young people who have been sexually assaulted is very confusing: be attractive, but to the right people at the right time and in the right place. This is true for both boy and girl children. They may need help to free themselves to be as they would like to be. They can never reclaim how they would have been had they not been abused, a source of much sadness. A child may fear not being believed or worry that they will get into trouble. We must remember the skill an abuser uses in manipulating the child into believing that he or she is at fault. This burden of complicity and shared culpability is very demoralising for any child. Fear of blame and disbelief are the main reasons children do not tell.

Often a child's desire to tell is a need to gain some control over a situation that has got out of control. To tell is to put your own needs above somebody else's: consequently, it takes a lot of courage. Frequently, following disclosure, the situation is no longer in the child's or the family's control. On the one hand, it can be a relief that someone else will take responsibility for what happens next; on the other hand, it is a public declaration of grave family failing. Each child will weigh up the circumstances when considering disclosing. They take into consideration a wide number of factors and often arrive at the conclusion that telling is too risky.

Children vary as to what they want to happen following disclosure. Most wish to remain with their families. Sometimes they want the perpetrator to leave what they see as an otherwise happy family. To

21

come into care and live separate to the rest of the family is usually the least preferred option. But children do not really get offered a wide range of options. Adult members of their family and adult workers make decisions and sometimes let the child know what options are left. Certainly the older a child the more they resent the lack of control they have over the fate of their lives. They may well resort to taking things into their own hands and 'place' themselves – with varying degrees of success.

Children who have been sexually assaulted learn more quickly than non-abused contemporaries that things are not always as they appear and that 'you can't always get what you want'. These are lessons in life that such a child learns most quickly and most painfully. They experience incomprehensible things and some of the reactions they are met with also defy explanation. In my experience, the prognosis is better for those children whose mothers believe them. If belief is withheld, then it casts very real doubt for the child on the value of having told. What are they then to make of their experience? Maybe they did imagine it? Maybe it won't happen again? Maybe it was an accident? Maybe they did something to make it happen to them? For a child who is being sexually abused, reality is sometimes worse than fantasy.

It is here, as a worker, that you can help a child or young person make sense of their experience. The conceptual model you use will dictate the manner of your response. There is a need to make some sense out of it. It is difficult to explain why one person did what they did to another person, especially if the perpetrator refuses to even acknowledge his actions, let alone take responsibility for them.

For the child who purposefully discloses, there is at least the beginning of an acknowledgement of what has been happening to him or her. That child, with help, can begin the process of recovery. Where sexual abuse is uncovered by workers, rather than divulged spontaneously by the child, that uncovering can be the beginning of a very painful experience of loss of control, separation and possible rejection. For all children, disclosure means giving up something that has been secret and opening up to the scrutiny of unknown people. Sometimes it is a gamble that does not pay off. As workers, we must try to ensure that the gains of disclosure outweigh the inevitable losses.

Issues for the family

In a family where sexual abuse is occurring, it is the breaking of silence that precipitates the crisis. As professionals, we rarely hear of the families where children are believed – where mothers have protected and fathers desisted. We need to recognise that some families have dealt effectively with sexual abuse without the state intervening.

It is also important to recognise that most children try and tell long before the statutory agencies become involved. A brief glance at the history of some of the young people reveals that warning signs or clues were often being given some time prior to disclosure. In telling, these children seek a response that confirms their sense of self-worth. Their desperation grows when important people – such as family members – fail to recognise distress signals, or misinterpret them. This is often what pushes a child to disclose to someone outside the family.

If a mother believes what her child says, she is confronted with the knowledge that her partner is a child molester and that she has failed to protect her child and to detect the episodes of abuse occurring in her household. If the child has disclosed to someone outside the family, she must also suffer the humiliation of the child not being able to tell her. These are all major blows to her self-esteem as a mother. As a believing parent, the mother must make moves toward protecting her child. Confrontation of the perpetrator is one of the methods used to resolve the problem. The mother, in this imaginary scenario, confronts the father, who typically denies the allegation. With a denial, the mother is thrown into confusion as to who to believe. She must make a choice: believe her child or her partner? It has to be recognised as one of the most difficult decisions a woman must make. It is often easier to disbelieve the child than confront the enormity of re-evaluating your family and marital relationships. We must also recognise the dependency, financial and psychological, that many women have in relation to their partners.

Child sexual abuse within the family is sufficiently serious as to destroy the integrity of the family unit. It will involve many members in the process of mourning – mourning the loss of intangible things like innocence, childhood, trust, images of happy families and perhaps tangible factors like loss of income, loss of child through reception into care, loss of partner through sentencing to prison.

The stakes then are very high for everyone when it comes to acknowledging what has been happening. If a chart is made of the potential gains and losses of each person in a family following disclosure of sexual abuse, most people can supply a long list of losses but would be hard pressed to see the gains.[6] Is it any wonder that families find child sexual abuse so hard to confront? As workers we need to be convinced of the gains to be made following disclosure, whatever our theoretical orientation might be.

We have referred to a 'family response' to sexual abuse. It is important to remember that families are made up of a collection of individuals; yet the family view may not be shared by each and every member of the family. It is as important to work with sub-systems as it is to work with the whole family: this means the siblings and the marital couple. In addition, the issues for the mother and the father (assuming he is the perpetrator) are different and will need individual work. One worker clearly cannot do all this work or be empathic to all the issues raised.

Typically, feelings range from anger at the mother for failure to protect and repugnance at the father's sexually inappropriate activities to sympathy for the target of the abuse. People generally prefer working with the target of the abuse. The older the child gets the less sympathetic we become. Over the age of 16 they are frequently abandoned to their fate. Workers, especially those in the caring professions, derive pleasure out of meeting people's needs: so, a needy child is particularly appealing. The difficulties set in when the child carries on being needy when they should be satisfied, or won't let us meet their needs; or they take what we give them without asking, or give it to someone else. Because the child has not learnt the same rules about giving and taking as you have, problems of this nature are bound to occur.

Working with mothers is the next preferred option. Mothers who believe their children are considerably easier to work with than mothers who do not. A mother who believes is considered to have made the right choice for her child. Mothers are supposed to choose things for other people, not themselves. A mother who continues to disbelieve her child would be considered unsuitable for a rehabilitation programme as she will be unable to protect that child in the future. Mothers need to be helped to believe and to see in that belief positive gains for every family member.

A believing mother often shows irrational feelings of anger towards the child, casting her as rival in her partner's affection. She will need an opportunity to discuss these feelings away from the child. Some mothers, too, were targets of sexual abuse, and this experience may have inhibited them from acting. They may have thought they were being over-protective and seeing too much in innocent interactions. Conversely, this can heighten their awareness and as a result they act swiftly and effectively to stop the abuse from occurring. It may be, however, that in the face of yet another powerful perpetrator, this mother is rendered impotent yet again. In some families the abuse of the mother, often in front of the children, is the first step of the abuser in establishing himself as the ultimate authority figure.

Working with perpetrators is frequently the least preferred option. Here you must confront all of your own assumptions about what the child molester looks like. Workers must recognise the deception involved in sexual abuse is often one of the most profound kinds of deceit as it is a deception of the self. Abusers convince themselves that they have not really done it. They will have construed events to make it seem that what they were doing was initiated by the child. They have blanked out any kind of appreciation for another individual to make it possible for them to do what they 'have' to do. Denial is not the same as lying. Denial is an unconscious |but active process of suppressing real, usually dreadful, events. So, it will not be obvious that the person is lying when they say they did not do it. Working with denial is extremely difficult as you have no platform on which to base your work: there is no recognition of a problem to work on.

A refusal to admit to perpetrating sexual abuse is a poor prognostic indicator. In the absence of a believing parent, a return home for the child should not be considered. Clearly, if a perpetrator admits to the abuse, the possibility for rehabilitation is available. However, we need to recognise how difficult it will be for a child to say, 'What I really want is for dad to go away'. Many young people cannot bring themselves to share their homes with their abusers. They often feel bitter that it is *they* who have to leave in the end. Nevertheless, we should equip young people with the skills they will need to deal with their family long after social services are no longer involved. Families who reject and disbelieve a child are capable of inflicting grievous psychic wounds long after the abuse has stopped.

It is also important to recognise that sexual offenders, like their targets, understand power hierarchies extremely well. In the presence of someone they believe to be more powerful than themselves (usually male professionals), they are frequently ingratiating, perhaps meek, or at least amiable. However, in the presence of those they consider less powerful than themselves (usually female professionals), they often display different characteristics such as threatening behaviour and sexual innuendo. This is a rare glimpse of the two faces of an offender: someone who is able to manipulate his presentation to suit his own ends. They fail even to recognise their duplicity.

Siblings rarely get a look-in. They are sometimes removed, sometimes not, when another sibling discloses. They can feel angry with that sibling for disrupting their lives. Knowledge that your father has sexually assaulted your sibling means you must re-evaluate your relationship with him and your opinion of him. Sometimes he may have abused more than one child in the family. The second child may remain quiet and watch what happens before making a decision about telling. Frequently such children decide to keep quiet. Because their way of coping was different, they may resent the actions taken by their sibling. Conversely, they may also tell together. Often one child is more motivated to tell, and the other reluctantly agrees to co-operate. Frequently it is this child who retracts or returns home, casting doubt on the veracity of the other child's disclosure and driving a wedge in the relationship between them – yet another betrayal.

For the children in the family who have not been abused, they may have to deal with the feelings of jealousy they had over the close relationship their sister had with their father. They may feel left out because they construed the abuse as a special favour, or guilty because they knew and did not tell anyone. Frequently, their feelings are not dealt with.

Perhaps what is most important about family issues in child sexual abuse is that most families, when confronted with this information, spend a lot of energy denying it, believing this to be the only way of keeping the family together. Often our interventions only serve to unite the family against the intruding outsider. When a family's integrity is threatened – and ironically this threat is always seen as coming from outside – each family member is forced to re-examine their membership. The major issue for the family must certainly be: can we continue together with this knowledge of ourselves? What seems the easiest solution is to deny the knowledge and supposedly maintain the integrity of the family.

The value of maintaining such a unit is highly questionable but it seems that many people – workers, parents and children – would rather cling to the appearance of normality than admit to their experience of perversity. In the absence of viable positive alternatives, there is often little choice.

References

1 Miller *Thou shalt not be aware: Society's betrayal of the child* Pluto Press, 1985.

2 Summit R 'The child sexual abuse accommodation syndrome' *Child Abuse and Neglect* 7, 1983.

3 This is an exercise used by myself and colleagues Anne Peake and Maria Mars on training workshops. We always start with the list of reasons not to tell before switching the frame.

4 Finklehor D *Child sexual abuse: New theory and research* New York: The Free Press, 1984, and *A sourcebook on child sexual abuse* Sage Publications, 1986 (in particular Chapter 10 'Boys as victims').

5 The author recognises that some mothers do know of abuse and do not stop it and in a minority of cases actually participate in sexually abusing their children. The mother who does not stop the abuse but knows of it is more closely related to the mother who does not know. The issues will be very similar but her self-esteem much lower.

6 Again, this is an exercise used by myself and colleagues Anne Peake and Maria Mars in training workshops.

5 Prognosis for rehabilitation after abuse

Dr Arnon Bentovim, Anne Elton and Marianne Tranter

Defining possible outcomes

When seeing families where breakdown is threatening or has occurred, we have found it helpful to make an overall assessment of the family and to attempt to define the possible outcome of our therapeutic work. To some extent this will influence our recommendations to a social services department or to a court about the prospects of work with the family. We have found it helpful to formulate the likely prognosis in the terms of:
– families for whom we think it likely that work for rehabilitation might succeed
– families for whom we think it doubtful that work for rehabilitation would be successful but where there are either some real grounds for optimism or perhaps insufficiently strong grounds to justify a category of hopelessness
– families for whom we think there can be no hope of rehabilitation.

Hopeful outcome
We can predict a hopeful outcome when:
1. The adults in the family take responsibility for their rejection of the child or for the state of the child and for their failure of care. They accept the need for treatment within a specific context, including separation if necessary, and recognise that they themselves need to change in some way in order to create a different and safer environment for the child.
2. There is some awareness that the responsibility thus accepted is held in the marital system; that is to say the acceptance is not based on one parent blaming the other entirely and the other taking full responsibility. Although we would emphasise the need for some real acceptance of responsibility by the adults, this is not to say that at the outset we would necessarily expect to see any genuinely felt grief and shame at the hurt caused the child. This would be, in our view, an unrealistic expectation at this beginning stage when the family is likely to be involved in some kind of battle with the professionals.
3. The children's needs are acknowledged as being primary and the parents' behaviour confirms this acknowledgement. For example, they may for a time live separately so that the abusing parent is at least temporarily removed from the child. In addition, there should be no scapegoating or blaming of a particular child, regardless of any real difficulties which that child might present.

4. We would regard it as hopeful if no other family members, including siblings or grandparents, expressed blame or scapegoated a victim. If other family members do scapegoat a particular child, they may well be expressing not only their own views, but also the real, but not openly acknowledged, feelings of the parents.
5. We need to observe some possibility of change in the patterns of interaction within the wider system and the potential for change even in rigidly held beliefs and attitudes.
6. If attachments are clearly alive, and there is potential for secure attachment between parents and child, we can be optimistic. We must qualify this statement for cases of child sexual abuse. Attachments may sometimes be very strong and real between victim and perpetrating parent (albeit probably ambivalent) but here their strength may constitute a negative indication.

Doubtful outcome
By far the largest group in our experience falls into the category of doubtful outcome. Indeed, the group is so large that it could be subdivided into a) doubtful, but with some real optimism, and b) very doubtful indeed, but without strong enough grounds to justify hopelessness.

The predictive factors are:
1. There is apparent uncertainty about whether the parents are taking full responsibility for the state of the child or for a particular form of abuse. For example, in sexual abuse a parent might say 'of course it was my responsibility but she was so cuddly'. The parental acceptance of the need for treatment will be at best ambivalent. Parents may strongly oppose some of the contextual conditions (like temporary separation of parents or of child from the perpetrating parent) and may not recognise that there is a primary need to change in some way themselves. Their opposition to statutory action may be bitter and intense, as opposed to a normal opposition based on the need to establish their parenting rights and their wish to be perceived as continuing parents.
2. There is either lack of recognition that the responsibility lies within the way the partners in the marriage interact: instead both or one may blame the other bitterly; or alternatively there may be a real sense in which they make the victimised child the scapegoat.
3. Children's needs are not easily recognised as primary. The adults may continually, or even periodically but strongly, put their own needs as dominant, overlooking the children' contradictory needs. For example, a mother may say, 'I don't

This article first appeared in *Adoption & Fostering* 11 1, 1987.

believe that it is a family without a man in it. I couldn't bear that and if that happened the children would have to go elsewhere.'

4. Children remain unsure, attachments are ambivalent and continue to be anxious. If statements are made like the one above, that is one way in which attachment is bound to be kept anxious. There may be evidence that there has been inadequate care and protection from the main attachment figures for a long time. Anxious attachments and 'frozen' attitudes in the parents' presence may show this, as may histories of neglectful parenting.

5. There is apparently limited potential for change in communication, affective status, boundaries, alliances and competence. That is to say family patterns appear rigid rather than healthily flexible. Scapegoating is a commonly observed response and likely to be part of a pernicious pattern. Even if the parents do not actively make the child a scapegoat, there is a risk that other family members may do so.

6. Relationships with the helping professionals may reflect the ambivalence, mirroring the swing between clinging and rejection which is evident in the parent/child relationship. Access is not likely to be very well used (either missed on occasion or unnecessarily curtailed) and similarly the families may be unreliable about allowing professional access to themselves.

Hopeless outcome

1. In this group the parents either totally or significantly deny any responsibility for the child's state. Instead the child is blamed and/or rejected outright. In addition the professionals who are attempting to help are blamed and their offers of work are refused, or seriously undermined.

2. There is no sense in which the children's needs are recognised at all by the parents. Even if the parents do strongly express a wish to keep an active relationship going between them and the children, the wish can clearly be seen as an expression of parental need rather than as meeting the children's needs.

3. Attachment is either extremely ambivalent or, more likely, avoidant. Access is poorly taken up, contact is perfunctory and there is no response if help is offered towards change.

4. The parents have failed to show appropriate concern for, or even to acknowledge, long-standing problems within the family: for example, drug addiction, alcoholism, promiscuity or severe psychiatric illness. Treatment has often not even been sought.

5. On the various paradigms of family relationship (communication, affective status, boundaries and alliances, parenting competence), there is evidence of breakdown. In addition, relationships with professionals remain at breakdown point, despite intensive investigation during assessment.

Making the assessment

It is important to make such an assessment, based on a broad view of how the family functions, since it is essential that we look carefully at the children's needs in family breakdown. If we feel hopeful, or if there are any grounds for optimism, we always try to work actively with a family towards the possibility of rehabilitation before considering long-term alternative parenting, whether fostering or preferably adoption.

There are many issues to be weighed concerning the individual child: the extent of the abuse in terms of its severity; the age of the child in terms of his or her ability to wait for an appropriate period while work for rehabilitation takes place; and the resources of the professionals who have to do the work. We have been convinced by our clinical experience that some families can only be rehabilitated when living in a residential placement or intensively supervised in day care. This is because of the level of anxiety about the extent of abuse and therefore the need to protect the child.

Such facilities and resources are not available in all areas which may be a limiting factor. The attitudes and views of the professionals (social work, psychiatric, paediatric and community health) in the particular area should also be considered and those of the political groups concerned with child care policies. It might be possible to place professional networks into similar categories as families in terms of their abilities and resources to meet family problems at different levels of severity.

When we look at the assessment of the family, we find it helpful to think about a number of issues:

1. Accepting responsibility for abuse and neglect

We see this as one of the most important factors for making a prognosis. The adult who has been responsible for the injury should be able to accept responsibility for the state of the child. Such acceptance of responsibility may be shown by grief and shame but we recognise that these emotions are very rarely present early in the process following the discovery of what may have been a long period of abuse. The process by which they so often see the child as the cause, justifying continuing abuse, initially shuts out a sense of grief and shame. Acceptance may be better judged by the parent's awareness that there is a need for the child to be protected, that separation may be necessary, that treatment is essential, and that there has to be a change to create a different and safe environment for the child.

In making assessments of the degree of responsibility taken by the adult(s), we have found it very helpful to use the techniques of the neutral position and circular questioning, as described by the Milan group.[1] By neutral stance we mean that if parents are unsure of the attitude of the questioners, and so find it hard to give a response to fit what they think the questioners want to hear, they will be helped to reveal their true attitude on the issue of responsibility. The technique of circular questioning relies on cues from the interviewed person being used to help to formulate the next question from the interviewer. It works in a to and fro manner but all questions have to be directed towards testing a particular hypothesis about the issue being discussed.

Thus, a father who had been convicted of severe physical abuse of his step-daughter, which included some sexual abuse, maintained quite solidly that although on the night she had been abused he had indeed punished her, in no way could he possibly take responsibility for the amount of bruising, fractures and sexual abuse that occurred. Indeed, he said that he had sought his solicitor's advice about trying to have his court sentence, a fine, reviewed on appeal. His solicitor after consulting counsel informed him that if he tried to appeal against his sentence, he might instead of the fine actually be sent to prison. When asked what he thought would happen to his marriage if he fully and absolutely took responsibility for the very clear-cut pattern of injuries to his step-daughter, he said categorically that he was certain then that his wife would leave him.

In another case a father, who it was alleged had sexually abused his daughter, made it clear that if he acknowledged responsibility for the abuse and had to go to prison, he was afraid (having been in prison before and in his own words 'administered punishment' to sex offenders) of what he knew would happen to him. In no way therefore would he take any responsibility. A common comment is that if responsibility is taken, then the individual may not be able to tolerate it and may even feel so suicidal that he actually kills himself.

Our experience is that people are only too well aware of what a failure to take responsibility means. Out of the circular questioning may come a conclusion that perhaps failure to take responsibility is a way of ensuring that someone else will take

action to protect and care for the child, and that this is perhaps what the parent wants at a very deep, unconscious level but cannot bring himself to say. A failure to take responsibility can thus be given a positive connotation and seen not as a denial of responsibility but as representing the parent's true sense of care for the child.

2. The degree to which responsibility is shared by both parents

It is essential in our view for successful rehabilitation that both parents take a share in the responsibility for the abuse or neglect of the child, even though one of the partners has to take the prime responsibility. In sexual abuse only the abuser can take direct responsibility and he may have to answer in court for the act. At the same time if the relationship between a mother and a child has been such that the child has not been able to confide in his or her parent for several years, this would indicate that both parents have to share the responsibility for the abuse. Similarly a parent who knows that the other parent is in a state of depression, anger or frustration and leaves that parent to care for the child, or ignores minor injuries or even major injuries over a prolonged period, also indicates a failure in sharing responsibility.

We are interested to know how much parents can share responsibility in this way, how much they blame the perpetrator, how great is the fear of sharing responsibility. For instance, one couple, after the mother had served a prison sentence for killing a child, were asked about the possibility of their three children returning to them. They made it clear that if they admitted responsibility for the death of the child, rather than blamed an intruder who they said must have come in and hurt the child whilst the family was asleep, then they could not trust themselves to have the other three children. At the same time they knew that if they did not take responsibility for the death of the child, then inevitably the court would take the view that they could not modify whatever had gone wrong to make the family a safe place in which the rest of the children could grow up.

This dilemma over responsibility is in our experience very frequent indeed, and as professionals we must be aware of the fact that some people feel completely blocked by it. If we take a neutral position, so that parents can express their confused views and feelings, we can ease the situation. We may, for example, try to indicate a difference between ourselves as individuals who understand their dilemma, compared with ourselves as professionals who have to be responsible to a court, our seniors, or our head of department. We might say, 'We understand now that we have reached a point in treatment when it must seem absolutely crazy for your daughter not to come back home, but what do you think the judge would expect us to do? Would he expect us to take the slightest risk with your daughter, or would he be expecting us to be cautious and to do things by slow stages?' (The parents' response in this case was to agree with the latter alternative. By this approach we are able to continue the process of helping the parents to take appropriate responsibility, or at least to recognise the inherent conflicts in the situation.)

3. Acknowledgement of children's needs

We are concerned to know whether parents acknowledge, not only in word but also in deed, that children's needs come first; that they accept, for instance, that the need for a child to live away may be more important and take precedence over a parent's need for the child. Again, it may be helpful to explore this by trying to define 'the difference between the attitude of parents who must want their child to be with them, as any parents would, and what a court or a social services committee would expect of parents who had found themselves hurting a child'. It is very important to establish whether the child is blamed or scapegoated as being the cause, branded as a liar or bad, evil in some way It is also essential to learn what the extended family's attitude is towards the child: 'always a bad one', 'always causing trouble'. Similarly the attitude of the extended family to the issue of the parents' responsibility for abuse is important. Expectation of their criticism or abandonment of them may well be another reason for not taking responsibility.

4. The acknowledgement of longstanding family problems

Research into predisposing factors of various kinds of abuse (Bentovim,[2] Oliver,[3] Lynch[4]) has indicated the inter-generational nature of abusive patterns within the family and the contribution of factors like personal illness, drug addiction and alcoholism. The attitude of the family towards such factors in their childhood, and also current states, is important to ascertain. Is there acknowledgement of and concern about these factors and whether treatment has been sought in the past? If not, what is their attitude towards these issues currently? Questioning around such issues, like 'What would the attitude of the court be towards your decision about whether you are going to do something concerning your drinking problem?' could be helpful. The history of the way treatment was used previously is important but it is

essential not to judge the future by the past as this will inevitably cause expectations to be confirmed.

5. The nature and rigidity of family patterns

Using the Family Description Format developed by the Family Studies Group at the Hospitals for Sick Children,[5] we find it helpful to view family patterns of interaction through a variety of frameworks. When looked at systematically they give a full picture of the nature of family interactions which predispose a family to breakdown. Family life and interactions are the ways in which individuals within families have their needs met, marital satisfaction is achieved and the children socialised, cared for and stimulated. Bentovim and Miller[6] have described the various family patterns which predispose to breakdown under various headings of family character (communications, affective status, boundaries and alliances); family competence in terms of ability to resolve conflict; the way the family operates in relationship to the environment, and finally the specific family process which leads to actual abuse.

A variety of approaches (many of which include tasks asking people to discuss topics with each other or control the children in an interview) gives information about the patterns in the family which are typical and which characterise it. It is hard to avoid such patterns for long when members of families are brought together face to face, particularly when some of the issues described previously are being looked at: for example, how specific abuse occured. There is thus some measure of the specific patterns and whether these can be shifted by particular modes of intervention. It is too easy to see highly destructive patterns as being prognostic in themselves. Our view is that the issue of primary importance is how rigid these patterns are and whether they can be shifted.

6. The nature of attachments and patterns of access

Through the work of Bowlby and others (for example, Main,[7] Ainsworth[8]), it is possible to delineate the attachment pattern within the family with greater accuracy than previously. There are now extensive descriptions of secure attachment and two forms of insecure attachment. The first is anxious attachment, which describes the clinging together of parent and infant that can appear as a good relationship in terms of seeking proximity, but which is a way of dealing with high degrees of anxiety about separation. The second is avoidant attachment. In this despite the best attempts of parent and child, there is avoidance of bodily closeness, poor eye to eye contact and a wooden character in their method of relating.

The pattern of attachments between different members of the family is of course important in terms of the different kind of attachment there may be between the child and each of the parents, between the children themselves, and within the extended family. Again it is important to ascertain whether abnormal attachments are rigidly fixed or can be modified by intervention.

The way that such attachments are shown through the pattern of visiting, if there is separation, is important, whether access is used regularly and for the full length of time, or perfunctory, broken and poorly maintained. Reasons for failure of access need to be looked at, as well as the response of the children before and after access. This describes the attachment for them in terms of their response to separation. A description of how people deal with separation gives important information about the nature of the relationships.

7. The relationships with care professionals

We are concerned to learn about the nature of the relationships with care professionals at present, whether there is a reasonable degree of co-operation or conflict and whether there is an attachment formed between them. We are interested in patterns of previous relationships with professionals. This helps us to see what relations with professionals may be like in future.

A parent who was himself or herself brought up in care, and who has a very good relationship with a previous social worker, may have formed the basis of a highly dependent relationship with a professional. On the other hand, a parent who was in care and who has vowed that his or her children will never be in care, might form a highly negative, rejecting form of contact. The ability of the professional involved to be able to resist 'scripts' and 'roles' is important here, and the nature of the professional organisation in contact with the family is important in terms of the availability of supervision, a wide variety of treatment approaches, and a management which is sympathetic to the notion of rehabilitation even in more worrying cases. Questions focused on what would the management of the organisation, the court, and other colleagues expect the professionals to offer, or how the professionals involved want the families to relate to them, will elicit helpful information. We can learn about current views and expectations and to distinguish between co-operation which is superficial or which has depth and potential for change.

Conclusions

The prognostic categories we have suggested are crude and there is scope during work with a family to change the prognosis. Unexpected factors may emerge in terms of the family's response to work, and new information may be discovered. We feel that it is essential that a fresh assessment is made of a situation, no matter how great the concern as far as the children are concerned and whatever the actual pattern of abuse or rejection. Subsequent work can be successful only if a realistic prognosis is made to form the basis of a contract for work. This will give the aims to be achieved, and the criteria for success as well as failure, and specify the consequences for the family and the professionals.

References

1 Palazzoli M S, Boscolo L, Cecchin G and Prata G 'Hypothesising – circularity – neutrality: three guidelines for the conductor of the session' *Family Process* 19, 3–12, 1980.

2 Bentovim A 'First steps towards a systems analysis of severe physical abuse to children in the family' in *First Report from Select Committee on Violence in the Family* Vol 3: Appendices 659–669, 1977.

3 Oliver J 'Some studies of families in which children suffer maltreatment' in Franklin A W (ed) *The challenge of child abuse* Academic Press, 1977.

4 Lynch M A and Roberts J *Consequences of child abuse* Academic Press, 1982.

5 Loader P, Burck C, Kingston W and Bentovim A 'Method for organising the clinical description of family interaction: the family interaction format' *Australian Journal of Family Therapy* 2:3, 1981.

6 Bentovim A and Miller L 'Family assessment in family breakdown' in Adcock M and White R (eds) *Good-enough parenting* BAAF, 1984.

7 Main M and Weston D A 'Avoidance of the attachment figure in infancy: descriptions and interpretations' in Parkes C M and Stevenson-Hinde J *The place of attachment in human behaviour* Tavistock, 1982.

8 Ainsworth M D 'Attachment: retrospect and prospect' in Parkes C M and Stevenson-Hinde J *The place of attachment in human behaviour* Tavistock, 1982.

Note: the ideas in this paper have been developed in Bentovim A, Elton A, Hildebrand J, Tranter M and Vizard E *Child sexual abuse within the family – assessment and treatment* John Wright, 1988.

6 Helping children who have been abused

Helen Kenward

Where do I start?

Child sexual abuse is like no other area of work and yet, like every other, it requires clear guidelines and procedures, good inter-agency co-operation, open support and supervision and, most importantly, acknowledgement by all concerned that the child has to have a voice and an advocate. The legal constraints mean that the professionals need to keep a clear head and prepare a good case both for child protection and keeping the options open for criminal proceedings.

Child sexual abuse leaves us feeling de-skilled and helpless, and with a variety of emotions based on our own experiences. It is important to be clear about these emotions and frame them appropriately before working with a child.

The child needs the adults to be strong, decisive and clear about their professional role. She does not need the worker to fall apart at the terrible things that have happened but to be receptive and understanding of her feelings. The child is asking for straight talking and for the abuse to stop.

The skills are there; we need to stop being afraid. Remember the child and the family; then wait and listen with all our senses.

The feelings engendered by listening to children who have been abused are very painful. The distress should be shared. The stress and burn-out dangers are high and the employing agency needs to recognise the worker's needs. There are a variety of responses beginning with good supervision and control over the number of cases an individual is responsible for. Consultation from an objective source is invaluable. In any area there may be a large number of agencies involved – Education, Health, Police, Probation, Social Services, NSPCC and Voluntary Organisations. Co-operation amongst the agencies will mean a large number of workers available for consultation with one another. Objectivity and not having responsibility for the case will mean helpful support and observations are available. Group support is very helpful; again, this can be multi-agency and will enhance the inter-agency communication. Work becomes easier when the teacher, police officer, police surgeon, social worker and paediatrician know one another and feel comfortable sharing difficulties.

When preparing to work with child sexual abuse, there are two important factors to consider – the individual worker and the professional network within which the individual operates. Because of the label 'sexual abuse', many workers lose sight of the fact that the child is still a child and that all the normal communication skills therefore apply. You still have to ask the child: what happened? Who did it? When and where?

Working with a child needs an understanding of the manner in which children tell of the abuse. The process of disclosure is one which needs a trusted adult prepared to enter the child's world, to listen and to facilitate the child's story being shared. It is important to remember that a crime may have been committed and that evidential material may be available that will help support the child's story. The professional network becomes important in terms of working together to prevent the child having to repeat a painful story too many times.

If a small baby sits on the floor, most adults will play – with a ball, with keys, or by finger games. Quickly the child responds with smiles and by joining in. These same responses are needed in age-appropriate ways when establishing communication with an abused child. Time is needed to reassure children, to find out what interests them and to begin to understand their stage of development. It is important to know the language they use and which members of the family and others are important to them.

How do you sensitise yourself without being deskilled and indecisive? It is most appropriate to work in a small group on the issues of types of abuse, the language children use, normal stages of development, signs and symptoms of abuse and our responses and experiences as part of a family and throughout life. Most people at some point in their lives have experienced a situation where they felt uncomfortable and were unsure how to respond, only later realising it might have had sexual connotations. The feelings engendered may well begin to explain the silence of children who feel guilty and worried about adult responses.

Jane was in the park when she was approached by a man who exposed himself. She ran away but did not tell her mother. Jane knew she would be angry because she had been told not to go to the park on her own. Jane didn't like the man's behaviour, was confused and distressed by him but could not share this because of her guilt. If you ask Jane about this experience it may well trigger the same feelings in her. It is important that the feelings are understood and contained, and don't get in the way of working with a child.

The skills, therefore, are listening, facilitating and observing. The child knows what happened. She was there. If we are talking, we are not listening – and we must keep a balance.

Child sexual abuse leaves a legacy for the survivors that can cause problems throughout their lives. It can present social workers and foster parents with a variety of problems when the child is in placement: sexualised behaviour, poor peer-group relationships, low self esteem, and a pre-occupation with sexual activity that leaves the child vulnerable to further abuse. It is vitally important to replace inappropriate sexual and other behaviour with normal behaviour, to improve social skills, to halt the sexualisation process and to help the child regain some of their lost childhood.

This may seem a daunting task but the great plus is that the child can grow very quickly and her capacity to learn is great. In deciding how to work, we need to start with the child. Working with pre-school children is very different from working with adolescents but the framework is the same. The manner in which the disclosure was made is an important consideration. For example, a child may have chosen a trusted adult and made a direct clear statement – like Melissa, who wanted her teacher to take control. She did not like what was happening and needed the teacher to make her safe: 'Last night my daddy made me watch him and mummy in bed.' Melissa first told at five but was not heard. By the age of seven her behaviour at school was so outrageous that she was rejected by everyone.

For many children, the direct approach fails since the adult does not want to hear the child, who then resorts to telling people through behaviour. The pattern may not be clear but the child expects us to understand: 'But I did tell, lots of times, but they didn't listen.' The child is labelled as difficult, disruptive and 'not very nice'. With luck the behaviour may bring adult attention which leads to disclosure. After disclosure, this behaviour pattern has to be changed as part of the work with the child.

However, the behaviour may result not in disclosure, but in the child being placed in care because she is 'out of control'. Such a child in placement may present many different problems. Often they settle well in care and vast improvements are noted; then trust leads to disclosure to the 'caring' adults ('feet under the table' syndrome).

Abuse may also become known as a result of third party statements, either by a witness or by a fellow participant. These are most difficult to resolve when they occur as part of a matrimonial dispute.

The most helpful response to a particular child will depend on other factors including the extent of the sexualisation, whether the child was coerced or seduced and the age of the child at the commencement and conclusion of the abuse. Consideration of these factors will allow us to prepare for and be consistent in our response. It must be recognised that much of the information will be given in little pieces. The child's experiences are like a giant iceberg and we only learn about what is below the water by establishing trust and confidence in the child. Therefore, we have to use observation and skills gained through experience.

Identifying and working with 'trigger' situations

Foster parents are excellent sources of information when trying to establish a starting point. Claire, aged five, on occasions would have hysterics on the stairs – covering her head, crying and kicking. Her distress seemed out of all proportion. Her skin became white with large red patches and she was inconsolable. Trying to untangle this pattern, we established that it was not when she had been naughty – in fact she could have been very happy minutes before. One consistent fact became clear: Claire was going up the stairs followed by the foster father. If she was at the top before he started up, she was fine, but if he was a couple of steps behind her this triggered hysterics.

Claire was helped to understand that her foster father was not going to hurt her. He would either go first or wait until she had reached the top. It was several days before she confided that 'daddy hurts on the stairs'. The abuse for Claire started when her birth father took her upstairs to the bedroom. She knew he was going to hurt her if he was immediately behind her. The foster father was able to correct this fear for her by understanding what was being triggered.

Knowing *where* the child was abused allows us to be careful not to unwittingly frighten her. This means the foster parents need to be explicit about who goes in which room, privacy and knocking on doors, all the time reinforcing that they are not going to abuse. The child needs to hear the adults say, 'I will do this and I won't do that'. Their actions are more likely then to be understood.

Bath-time is particularly important. For most people a bath is a warm comfortable experience. Children have toys and boats to play with and most of us have found ourselves playing with soap bubbles whilst pondering on the day's events! However, the child who has been abused in the bath may be terrified. Understanding that fear and correcting it will depend upon the age of the child. Susie objects violently to a 'normal' bath-time routine; however, at seven, she is old enough to wash herself. The foster parent can help her by describing how to wash, perhaps by letting her help with bath-time for a younger child or by mime. Talking through the routine night after night may feel tiresome but soon the child will be doing it for you: 'We put the water in, now the bubbles. Here's the towel and here's my nightie. Now mum goes to the linen cupboard, I get undressed, hop in, that's nice . . .'; and so the warmth and comfort at bath-time can become the normal experience. If the foster father is in charge, he can still supervise from the hall or bedroom and chat about nothing until the child feels safe. Triggers don't go away quickly – and sometimes never – but understanding them helps both the adults and the child. An older child may need and want the reassurance of a back wash or a hair wash that allows them to be the safe small child again – but always with permission and with the boundaries clearly stated. A baby or toddler may need to be washed in the basin or small bath and gradually graduate to the large bath. It is all very obvious in an unobvious way. The child who has been abused may be 15 months old or an adolescent but the child you are working with is the *hurt* child and inside feels very young and very afraid.

John, aged eleven, described it beautifully and with great perception. He had been for a weekend with his new foster parents: 'I liked them but they didn't know how I am inside. If I was a baby they would put me in a high chair, they'd change me if I was wet and they wouldn't expect me to walk. That's how I am. I don't know what they want me to do or how to do it and I'm afraid in case I make them angry and they hurt me.'

It may be that certain foods have been triggers or rewards for sexual favours. A child who turns white on being offered crisps may have no trouble with chocolate. It has to be remembered that adults frequently feel very guilty immediately after the abuse and wish to compensate for the hurt by giving some small treat, but the child would not have interpreted it that way, especially if it was accompanied by, 'Don't tell, it's a secret. It will hurt your mummy if you tell. I will go to prison if you tell.'

Anna, aged eight, described meal-times as very worrying. Food had been dependent upon her being sexually co-operative. When her foster mother offered her a plate of food she did not know what to do: 'I'm hungry and I want it. I can't make my hand take it.' We all talked about her need for food and ways of helping her, and we simply decided that *she* would serve the food. The plates were put on a trolley and Anna lifted them off for all the family. For some time she hid her plate with her arms in case it was removed before she had finished and all the members of the family learned not to touch her when food was around. Anna's food was placed where she could take it herself. The other children in the family were the first to get her to take anything from a hand.

Bed-time is a complicated minefield. A child who has waited for a nightly visit, who has only slept fitfully because of fear, will not have a good sleep pattern. Bed is not the warm safe place it should be and night-time presents many problems. Many foster parents will have experienced the child's need to stay up and talk, to be hyperactive once everyone has settled and only fall asleep exhausted in the early hours. Understanding the pattern of abuse allows a new routine to be developed and meanwhile makes the hyperactivity more tolerable for the carers.

Frances was abused by her father from the time she was nine until the age of 15. Her pattern of behaviour was very disturbed. The only time she was relaxed was between 11.00 a.m. and 3.30 p.m. Her father had abused her after school, after the pub and before school in the morning and she was in a state of high anxiety leading up to these times. She fell into a deep sleep around 3.00 a.m. and was impossible to wake in the morning. Frances had to learn the reasons for what was happening and that she was safe. At 19 she was still experiencing some difficulties but at least was beginning to make sense of why she was feeling that way. Whether and how she controlled it became her choice.

Helping children to move on, make their own choices and take appropriate control

Choice becomes a very important word when working with abused children. There comes a point in their healing when they have to learn that certain behaviours set them apart. This means that people label them and, what is worse, may re-abuse them. Often the behaviour is very subtle and the adults have to learn to be specific about helping to correct it. Posture and provocative behaviour have been taught and reinforced. It needs to be replaced with more appropriate behaviour. Kisses should be on the cheek, not on the mouth; cuddles at the side or facing away when on a man's knee, rather than straddled. Rubbing of the genitals through clothes has to be stopped not by rejection but by 'we don't do that, we do this'.

It is very important that children whose lives have been dominated by sexual activity or the fear of it learn how to enjoy normal things. Newly-acquired skills that can be praised will be a stepping stone which is rewarding for adult and child. Initially the skills should be those which are easily acquired – the clarinet or flute is difficult to learn but riding a bicycle or making pancakes are easy. Paddling a canoe means that the child is in charge of him or herself and simple movements produce a result. The range of possibilities is endless: 'Frances and I went sailing. The skipper handed her control of his yacht whilst the rest of the crew organised the sails. Our passage out of the harbour was smooth and without mishap. Frances's face was a picture of joy and concentration. For the rest of the day she was heard muttering, "I did it, he let me; his boat and I did it." Frances was in control of herself and others and a large yacht. Never before had such a message been given to her so strongly.'

Identifying triggers and skills are important, but equally important is learning to relate to other adults and peers. Many children have difficulties and cause embarrassment by, for example, approaching visitors with inappropriate behaviour. Masturbation is a common problem; a child whose body is used to touch and stimulation may respond to new situations by attempting to touch themselves or others. The child needs to know that although it is not wrong to masturbate it is inappropriate in public or with others and the energy needs to be gently directed to other activities. Learning what to do with your hands when you are unsure or bored is difficult. Knitting, crochet or model-making may seem a big jump but the child needs to be offered viable alternatives to inappropriate masturbation.

Behaviour in school can be a problem. Frances remembers sitting in class, aged eleven: 'The teacher was telling us the facts of life. I looked around the class and knew they were hearing it for the first time. But I'd done it. At playtime they were laughing and joking. I didn't know that dads didn't do that. I didn't know what to do and so I stopped talking. No one wanted to play with me because I didn't know how to without giving away the secret. What if someone guessed?' Frances's withdrawal was noticed and she was labelled shy and difficult. I asked her why she didn't tell any of the concerned adults around her. 'No one asked me', was her reply.

John was afraid to go into the showers in case anyone could tell his dad had buggered him. He was afraid to have a girlfriend in case he did not know what to do and in case she suspected.

Children like Frances and John need to be taught how to play and interact normally with peers of both sexes. They should be helped to discover that they don't have to wear a label which says 'victim'.

Abused children become more and more confused; adolescence is confusing enough without the added burden of inappropriate adult behaviour. When they are unsuccessful with their peers, abused children may seek adult company and comfort and may be abused again by adults with shaky boundaries, leaving a further burden of guilt since the child sought it. If children have enjoyed the physical contact, they miss it and feel guilty for enjoying an activity which everyone says was wrong. Melanie loved her dad. She enjoyed his touches. It was the only time she had any cuddles and she was angry when it stopped because her mother caught them. Labels of 'dirty' and 'bad'' made her very unsure. Explaining the rights and wrongs to a child is difficult but simple analogies help: 'You can ride a bicycle on the pavement but not on the road – it's not safe yet. When you're bigger you will be able to. If I put you in a car and showed you how to drive it you are clever enough to learn but your legs are not long enough to reach the pedals and you can't see over the wheel. It's dangerous although you might enjoy it. When you're older you can drive a car. When you're older you will find someone who loves you and it will be right to do these things your dad did.'

Variations on this theme will make sense to a child whose behaviour has to change. The time spent with a child learning to make sense of that behaviour and helping them correct it is very rewarding. If the explanations are clear and understandable then they can make the choice of removing the label 'victim' and replacing it with 'survivor'. Rewarding acceptable and appropriate behaviour and explaining unacceptable behaviour gives satisfaction for adult and child.

Questions and answers

Helen Kenward

1

If a child never mentions being abused, how do I handle it?

When the child arrives, the foster parent should say something like, 'I know that some difficult things have happened to you. You may want to talk about it sometime and when you're ready, we will listen.'

2

If a child talks all the time to everyone, how do I handle it?

Talk with the child about being the centre of a circle. In the circle are the people who know everything. In a second ring put in the people who know a little and in a third ring those who don't need to know. Each time the child begins to talk about it help him or her decide which ring they belong in. The drawing could be put somewhere prominent in order that the child be prompted to think out who should know and what.

3

How do I help to get a cover story together?

Using the above concept, develop a list of things about the child which he or she may or may not want others to know about, along with cut-off points for who knows what. I think the simpler the explanation the better. If a child feels really pressed by someone, then a statement such as, 'It's hard to explain and it's painful to talk about' will satisfy some. Teach the child diversionary techniques so that they are not left in a difficult spot. In the final analysis, the child has to decide what he or she want others to know.

4

How do I address the issue in the life story books?

I would write a letter to the child explaining my involvement and the process of disclosure and work with the family. I would put this in an envelope (copies need to be kept!) at the back of the book or somewhere safe so that the child has control over who sees it.

5

How do I deal with my horror and pain in front of the child?

The child needs you to be strong and take the pain without showing any signs of rejection. In private you should handle it in the way appropriate for you. Stamp, swear, throw or punch a pillow, tear up paper or do the household task you like least — for me, washing up! Be prepared for a physical response. I find it hard to eat or keep any food down sometimes after a disclosure: it's my body telling me that I'm dealing with painful difficult things — don't deny it. Find the right person for you to talk to. But *be strong* for the child — they have had such courage and they need us to respond similarly.

6

How do I discuss the future, particularly if the prognosis is poor?

It is important to remember that the child may have mixed feelings about the offender and, therefore, we must be careful not to be critical but to help the child retain any positives they can. I always try to find at least one good thing that happened so that when things look really bad I can say, 'Well, he did buy you a packet of crisps,' and the child is left feeling that there was something positive about the relationship.

7 Fostering the sexually abused child

Jacquie Roberts

In the 1980s an increasing number of children are being referred for fostering after being identified as sexually abused. At the same time, people are becoming more open to the idea that a child might have been sexually abused and therefore more children in care are being recognised as such. The consequence for foster parents is that they are asked to care for a child who is not only suffering from separation and loss, but also from the serious results of having been sexually abused. Many skilled foster parents have come to terms with dealing with abused and neglected children, but when the abuse has been of a sexual nature the problems are even more complex. I have heard many a parent say sympathetically that they can understand how child abuse can occur – 'There but for the Grace of God go I' – but I have yet to hear the same comment made about sexual abusers. Sexual abuse is frightening and abhorrent to most people.

I am writing this paper in response to foster parents (and prospective adopters) who have asked what they can do to help a child who has been sexually abused. The first step is to face the fact that child sex abuse does occur. The next step, which is by far the hardest, is to accept how often child sex abuse occurs. Estimates vary, but Baker and Duncan[1] have recently conducted an epidemiological survey in association with the MORI organisation which has indicated that at least one adult in 10 was sexually assaulted as a child. The perpetrator of that act is most likely to have been known to the child. The majority are members of the family. If this is the rate for child sex abuse in Britain, then there are adult sexual abusers among our colleagues, friends and maybe even family.

The problems a sexually abused child brings to the foster home

The many problems a sexually abused child may bring to a foster home will not simply be the result of the sexual assault. The results of the abuse depend on many variables. Obvious considerations are the age of the child; the age difference between child and abuser; the nature of the abuse and its frequency or duration. Most important, the relationship between the child and abuser makes all the difference to the child's reaction. It could be that an isolated sexual attack by a stranger, although terrifying at the time , will not have such a devastating effect on a child's world as chronic, albeit very gentle, sexual interference by someone the child has trusted as a father figure for years.

Just as important is the amount of secrecy surrounding the abuse. If children are threatened and made to keep the abuse secret from the adults they trust, they have lost their security and trust in any adults. Finally, the after-effects of sexual abuse for a child may have little connection with the actual abuse, but rather be a result of the way the disclosure of the sexual abuse was handled.

Possible consequences of disclosure

The first thing that can happen to sexually abused children is that their story is not believed. It is easy to imagine how this destroys their faith in adults, especially if the person who does not believe them is their mother. Next, the child may be subjected to a medical examination which is frightening and unpleasant if it is not extremely well handled. This medical examination may be more physically intrusive than the abuse itself. The child may then be made to repeat the story of the abuse over and over again to different people, some of whom may be seen by the child to get some excitement out of what they are hearing. A serious consequence for many children is that they are taken away from home and they witness their family breaking up. They feel responsible. Such a feeling is reinforced by the abuser and other members of the family blaming the child and saying, 'Look at what you have done now.' This blaming, and the fact that children know that people are talking and whispering about them, result in thcm feeling bad and as though they deserved to be abused in the first place. All this can make children behave in such a way that they almost invite further abuse as a way of confirming for themselves how bad they are.

Behaviour problems in younger children

Many different behaviour problems have been attributed to child sexual abuse but, as with the behaviour problems found in physically abused children, no firm statements can be made about cause and effect. It is worth considering some of the behaviour difficulties so that foster parents can at least know what they might expect and understand more about why the children behave as they do.

The biggest problem for foster families, especially those with other young children in the home, is sexual acting out by these children. It is a disturbing and sometimes repulsive sight to see very young children simulating sexual intercourse. In addition, it is quite common for sexually abused children to suffer from serious sleep disturbance and frightening nightmares: in the past, sleep might not have provided the safe comfort it usually does. Eating disorders are common in fostered children. Sexually

This article first appeared in *Adoption & Fostering* 10 1, 1986.

abused children can show their hurt through refusing to eat anything or through over-eating grossly. Bodily disorders have also been noted. Complaints about all sorts of aches and pains, bowel and bladder problems, again expected in distressed foster children, have been related to the previous sexual abuse. Clearly some sexually abused children lose all their trust in adults and become frozen or withdrawn; some even become completely mute, as vividly described by Maya Angelou.[2]

Even in very young sexually abused children one can observe the beginnings of promiscuous behaviour. The children will go to anyone, including complete strangers, and demand physical contact and flaunt their bodies in a sexual manner because this has brought them rewards in the past. Because these children are often on their mettle, wondering what to expect next, just like battered children, they become distractible, finding it hard to concentrate, and this produces problems for them in school.

Finally, some sexually abused children feel so badly about themselves that they take it out on their own possessions and even their bodies by cutting things up or cutting their skin with sharp instruments.

Behaviour problems in older children

Children over the age of 10 or 11 can be even more difficult to deal with when they have been sexually abused. Because of their age they may seem more blameworthy for their part in the abuse. I have heard people say things like 'She's that sort' or 'She asked for it, you know'. Added to the list of earlier problems, which can still occur in older children, are anorexia or the opposite, bulimia nervosa. Sexual promiscuity is an obvious consequence because these teenagers have not learnt how to get close to people in any other way. Understandably, sexually abused teenagers have been noted for their anger at what has happened to them and if they have no opportunity for therapeutic help after the abuse, they can so easily act out their problems in the usual delinquent ways: absconding, stealing and indulging in drug and alcohol abuse. Hysterical seizures have been thought for a long time to be a consequence of sexual abuse.[3] Much more commonly teenagers can feel so bad about themselves that they become depressed and even make suicide attempts. A general problem for all these children is that they feel so different from other children of their age that they isolate themselves from their peer group and find it very hard to make friends.

The child in the foster home

Sexually abused children arrive in the foster home with the emotional damage inflicted on them not only by the abuse but also by the consequences of the discovery of the abuse. They enter the foster home upset at being separated from familiar adults and places. They feel punished and blamed for everything that has happened and yet they crave affection from a parent whom they can trust. On top of this they are likely to resort to sexual behaviour to test out the foster parents or as a form of comfort. They are likely to reveal considerable knowledge about sex that can shock even the most experienced foster parents. Above all, they are isolated from other children and desperately need friends.

The immediate problem for the foster parents is their emotional reaction to what has happened to the child. There is shock, fear, disbelief and for some people, if they are honest, sexual abuse of children rouses some sort of excitement and prurient interest.[4] These responses would be easier to deal with if the professional helpers were not so anxious and uneasy themselves about the subject of child sexual abuse. The foster parent is less likely to receive firm and confident guidance about a sexually abused child than in other cases.

The whole episode may evoke for both the social workers and the foster parents memories of a childhood sexual assault of their own which they may have suppressed. Seeing even very young children with sophisticated sexual knowledge may raise questions for the foster parents about their own attitudes to sex. Infertile adoptive couples may be particularly vulnerable because of the close relationship between their sexuality and infertility. A more devastating problem for some foster parents is to see the effect the sexually abused child's story has on their own children. They have the dilemma of deciding how much their children should know to understand the child and how little they should know in order not to label the child further.

A central part of the foster parents' job is to talk to and about the birth parent. This is difficult enough with a battering or neglectful parent, but it is especially difficult when it involves a sexually abusing parent. It is also hard not to blame the non-abusing partner if they 'let the sexual abuse happen'.

Problems in the foster home

The most immediate problem for many foster families is that the sexually abused child may teach other children in the home sexual play. Very young children may be particularly vulnerable to being interfered with. At the other extreme, older children in the home may be invited and provoked into a sexual relationship which they do not understand. Careful matching of children with families is needed to avoid compromising young teenagers.

Visitors, neighbours and friends can cause difficulty. How much should you explain about why the child is with you? It is surely fairer to the child to make up a 'cover story'? And yet, some physically demonstrative friends may need to be warned off affectionate gestures because it could give the child wrong messages. Members of the extended family, like grandparents, may know more but may find it hard to act naturally with the child and some may even avoid physical contact. One foster parent said to me that one of her biggest responsibilities with a sexually abused child is to educate other people. Finally, it is not rare for foster parents to have visitors who take an unnatural morbid interest in the child and these people have to be dealt with firmly.

Foster parents, too, can find themselves compromised. What can start off as an innocent game of hide and seek could end up with the child expecting sexual contact in a dark corner. A much more aware attitude to body messages and to sexual behaviour has to develop to avoid giving the child the wrong messages. The consequence is, however, that foster parents may feel they are becoming sex-obsessed and prevented from acting naturally in their own home. For example, rules about bath time and nudity in the home may have to change. Any foster parents of an older child who has been sexually abused must know that there is a risk of allegations being made against them.

This leads to the final problem for all of us involved in fostering and adoption work. If the rate of child sexual abuse is as high as suggested, it must be happening in some foster homes at the moment. We all have a responsibility to be more open about the subject, follow up suspicions and maybe search within ourselves for any possibility of acting on sexual feelings towards children.

How the foster parent can help

First and foremost foster parents need to sort out their inner reactions to the problem and talk openly about it to their partners and close family. Next, and most important for the child, they need to remove any blame from the child. If they continue to think that the child is inviting the abuse and believing it is partly their fault, they will never help the child change his or her behaviour.

Several foster parents have stressed how important it is to put the sexual abuse into perspective, to think of the child as a whole and to work on all the other problems the child has. If the sexual abuse is stressed too much, it becomes an obsession for everyone and can hinder normal development and relationships. Most important for

the children is to help them feel good about themselves. Their self image and self esteem need careful building so that they have other areas in life that make them feel good. They need to know they are wanted and liked for reasons other than sex. If the sexual play is overt and continuing, they need to be taught about privacy, normal sexual behaviour and about being able to say 'no'. Michele Elliott has written a helpful book explaining how to teach children to avoid sexual abuse.[5] In it she stresses the need to teach the difference between good and bad secrets and for children to know that they are in charge of their own bodies. What is particularly attractive about her book is that it is aimed at all children, not just those labelled a problem.

Some sexually abused children need firm help and guidance about changing unconscious sexual behaviour and giving out sexual signals. They need to hear about the serious consequences of what they are doing. This is difficult in the current culture of western societies where for teenage girls the ethos is that it is good to be pretty and sexy. On the other hand, many sexually abused children, even those who have not been seriously hurt, need constant reassurance that their bodies have not been damaged by the abuse, that they are not dirty or different, and that other people do not know what has happened to them simply by looking at them.

The long-term strategy is to concentrate on helping these children to make good relationships with children of their own age. This builds up self-confidence and protects them. An isolated child who only makes relationships with adults is bound to be more at risk of assault. It is only through learning to get on with their peer-group that they will learn how to make good emotional and sexual relationships when adults. The long-term consequences of child sexual abuse can be serious psychiatric illness or an unhappy partnership with an abusive spouse and parent. We have a responsibility to prevent this for all the sexually abused children in our care.

References

1 Baker A W and Duncan S P 'Child sexual abuse – a study of prevalence in Great Britain' *Child Abuse and Neglect* Vol 9 No 4, 1985.

2 Angelou M *I know why the caged bird sings* Virago, 1984.

3 Freud S 'Some general remarks on hysterical attacks' in Strachey J (ed) *The standard edition of the complete psychological works of Sigmund Freud* Vol IX Hogarth Press, 1909.

4 Jones D P H and McQuiston M 'Interviewing the sexually abused child,' Vol 6 Kempe Center Series, Henry Kempe Center, University of Colorado School of Medicine, 1205 Oneida St, Denver, Colorado, US, 1985.

5 Elliott M *Preventing child sexual assault*, Bedford Square Press, 1985.

Tread with care: fostering sexually abused children

Kala Nobbs and Barbara Jones

The task of fostering sexually abused children can be especially difficult and demanding. There are many stress factors and foster families are vulnerable to marital and intra-familial conflicts as well as problems with neighbours and friends.

We talked to several sets of foster parents and the following experiences are not untypical.

John and Mary fostered Sally, aged 15, who made an allegation that their adult son had had sex with her while visiting the family home. The foster parents were both amazed by this allegation but responded in different ways.

John felt Sally should be believed. Mary was astonished that John didn't trust their son and felt John had been 'seduced' by Sally's 'sweet and lovely' nature. John was 'hopping mad' when the child was removed at Mary's request, and felt angry with his wife for being too hard on Sally. He felt they 'should have coped' and given Sally the therapeutic help she needed.

Polly and Mike fostered Tanya, aged 13, who had been sexually and emotionally abused in her home and also raped vaginally and anally by a stranger. Efforts to integrate Tanya into the local community were fraught with problems. Tanya told neighbours and school friends about her abuse. They didn't know how to cope and were embarrassed by her revelations and her sexualised behaviour.

When Tanya went to Guide camp she instigated some sort of sexual activity (combined with threats) among the girls in her tent. As a result, she was sent home. Some of the Guides' parents were angry and abusive towards the foster parents and demanded the social services department remove Tanya from the neighbourhood.

In addition to the sort of risks cited above, foster parents are twice as likely as the general population to abuse their children,[1] and are also more likely to be victims of false allegations.[2]

We know that children who have already been the victims of abuse are vulnerable to re-abuse. Sometimes sexually abused children have received positive reinforcement – cuddles, rewards, 'love', attention – for their sexual passivity and behaviour, often from an early age. They may have developed coping mechanisms in these difficult family situations which they try to introduce into their relationship with their new carers.

This behaviour, which was pleasing to their abusers, may be demonstrated towards the foster father or visiting relatives and friends. Some foster parents take advantage of this and further sexually abuse their foster child.

Other carers find the strain of coping with sexualised behaviour too great and abuse their foster child either emotionally or physically.

Children whose abuse has left them afraid of men, or extremely clinging, withdrawn, with eating/sleeping problems; children who reject cuddles and comfort, or misunderstand the intention and scream and cry, may unwittingly contribute to a situation where further abuse occurs.

A recent American study[3] showed a rate of *substantiated* allegations of abuse (all types) by foster parents which varied from two to 18 per 1,000 foster homes. The rate for the general population is roughly half this figure.

Consequently, we cannot assume that foster children are lying when they make allegations against their foster parents. We cannot assume that children like the attention they receive from making an allegation. In fact, children who have already disclosed abuse will know it can be an extremely distressing experience.

We must avoid the trap of having double standards where foster parents are concerned and remember that only a very small number of sexual abuse allegations made by children are false.

How, then, does this tie in with the information from a 1986 study[4] which found that one in six foster parents interviewed had faced an abuse allegation and that all had been cleared following investigation? It seems that, while a small number of foster parents are more likely to abuse their foster children, foster parents are far more likely than other people to have unsubstantiated complaints laid against them.

It is therefore essential that, as a service dependent on the goodwill of volunteers, we learn how to deal with allegations in a fair and sensitive manner.

If sexual abuse were alleged, we would make the following broad recommendations:
– that allegations are dealt with in the social services department's child abuse procedures
– that foster parents are informed at an early stage of what has happened, what the implications are, what they can expect from the social services department and the respective roles of social worker and fostering officer
– that the allegation is dealt with by a senior manager who is not the social worker's line manager and does not know the foster parents, but does know about fostering and the dynamics associated with sexual abuse.

It is important that the different roles of social worker and fostering officer are fully understood by

This article first appeared in *Community Care* in June 1988 and is reprinted here with permission.

the professionals, the family and the foster child, when an allegation is made.

The social worker's main task should be to support the child and to deal with the procedural issues generated by the allegation. The fostering officer can operate as the link between the social services department and the foster parents, but it is crucial that the foster parents are told that fostering officers are unable to offer unconditional support.

They are employed by the investigating social services department and will not be able to keep confidences. They will be called on to make comment at meetings, case conferences and even court hearings.

The purpose is not to protect foster parents who abuse their foster children but to ensure that social services departments recognise the potential stress of some of the placements we make, and that they take all possible precautions to protect both children and foster families.

We hope there will be debate about possible dilemmas involved in fostering sexually abused children and that social services departments clarify for social workers, fostering officers and foster parents the likely procedures in instances or allegations of sexual abuse.

Ways foster parents can help protect themselves

1. Keep a written log, noting all incidents, however trivial
2. Participate in training
3. Share any incidents or feelings which make you feel uncomfortable, with your support worker
4. Family members should think about their family patterns of behaviour (such as nudity, privacy, play, secrets, washing, touching) and identify situations which might be misinterpreted
5. Be aware that, when fostering a child who is behaving in a very sexualised manner, male family members need to be careful of the situations they become involved in – not putting themselves at unnecessary risk of being misunderstood by the child – though it is important to keep things in perspective and to maintain a normal family life
6. Encouraging open channels for honest and free discussion between yourselves and the children. It is important that your own children feel able to tell you if the foster child tries to involve them in sexual activity
7. Being actively involved with your local National Foster Care Association group which may provide

further training and advice and offer support if the going gets tough

Ways in which social services departments can minimise risk to foster parents

1. Recognise the stress and impact fostering sexually abused children can have on a family
2. Provide clear guidelines and role definitions relating to sexual abuse
3. Provide training for foster parents (if possible pre-placement) which encourages open communication about difficult issues, such as sex and personal relationships
4. Make sure all such placements have a written agreement which makes clear statements about:
– the procedures which will happen in the event of an abuse allegation
– the aims, objectives and length of placement
– the therapeutic plan and the foster parents' role in this
– a plan for respite care
5. Ensure the foster parents receive as much information as possible about the child's background and the precise nature of the abuse
6. Offer a high level of placement support which must include regular visits by the foster parents' support worker. Foster parents should be encouraged to share incidents or concerns, however vague, with their fostering officer as this may provide crucial evidence in the future. Foster parents need to feel part of the care team and to know that their feelings and opinions are valued
7. Provide realistic financial remuneration to cover other respite care, babysitting and so on. Recognise the additional work and risks involved in such placements

References

1 McFadden and Ryan *Abuse in family foster homes* East Michigan University, 1986.

2 Nixon S, Hicks C and Ells S 'Support for foster parents accused of child abuse' *Foster care*, December 1986.

   Nixon S and Hicks C 'Experiencing accusations of abuse' *Foster care*, December 1987.

3 See 1 above.

4 See 2 above.

Note: readers may be interested to know that Stephen Nixon and colleagues at the University of Birmingham are undertaking some research into false allegations of sexual abuse against foster parents (see reference 2 above). The results will be published in *Adoption & Fostering*.

Bibliography

Recommended reading

Finkelhor D *Child sexual abuse: new theory and research* Collier Macmillan, 1984.

Finkelhor D (ed) *Source book on child sexual abuse* Sage, 1986.

Mrazek P and Kemp C H (eds) *Sexually abused children and their families* Pergamon, 1981.

Glaser D and Frosh S *Child sexual abuse* BASW, 1988.

Haugaard J and Reppucchi D *The sexual abuse of children*, Jossey-Bas, 1988.

Sgroi S M *Clinical intervention in child sexual abuse* Lexington Books, 1982.

Bentovim A and Tranter M 'Child sexual abuse within the family' *New England Journal of Medicine*, 1st edition, March 1988.

Bentovim A and Tranter M 'Sexual abuse – incest victims and their families' *New England Journal of Medicine*, 2nd edition, November 1988.

Books for children

Fay J and Flerchinger B *Top secret: sexual assault information for teenagers only* USA: King County Rape Relief, Renton, Wa, 1981.

Adams C et al *No is not enough: helping teenagers avoid sexual assault* USA: Impact Publishers, 1984.

Elliott M *Preventing child sexual assault: a practical guide to talking with children* Bedford Square Press/ NCVO, 1985.

Hart-Rossi J *Protect your child from sexual abuse* USA: Parenting Press Inc, 1984.

Freeman L *It's my body: a book to teach young children how to resist uncomfortable touch* USA: Parenting Press Inc, 1982.

Wachter O *No more secrets for me* Puffin, 1986.

Fay J *He told me not to tell* USA: King County Rape Relief, Renton, Wa, 1981.

Atkinson L, Kemp-Keller L and Dawson B *I belong to me* Canada: Whortleberry Books, 1984.

Further reading

Spring J *Cry hard and swim* Virago, 1988.

Angelou M *I know why the caged bird sings* Virago, 1983.

McNaron T and Morgan Y *Voices in the night* USA: Cleis Press, 1982.

Riley J *The unbelonging* The Women's Press, 1985.

Walker A *The color purple* The Women's Press, 1983.

Videos

Mainly for children

"What ta-do" EMI Education Media International.

"Strong kids – safe kids" National Children's Bureau.

"Kids can say 'No'" Rolf Harris Videos.

"Feeling 'Yes' Feeling 'No'" EMI Education Media International.

Mainly for teenagers

"You can say 'No'"

"Crime of violence"

Both produced by Newcastle Theatre Company and distributed by Albany Videos.

Video material mainly for training purposes

"Breaching the silence" Joyce Morrison and David Will.

"Challenging myths" David Will, Jacquie Roberts and Joyce Morrison.

Available from: Macmed, 6 Douglas Terrace, Dundee, Scotland DD3 6HN.

The Training Advisory Resource for Child Sexual Abuse at the National Children's Bureau is compiling a database on available training materials, including videos.

Enquiries are welcome on: 01-278 9441 or at: TAGOSAC, National Children's Bureau, 8 Wakley Street, London EC1V 7QE.

Also useful is the National Foster Care Association's information pack on child sexual abuse.

For details, contact: NFCA, Francis House, Francis Street, London SW1P 1DE (tel 01-828 6266).